D1236855

THE ROSES RACE AROUND HER NAME

Poems from Fathers to Daughters

The cover photograph is of Alice Liddell, prototype for *Alice In Wonderland*, by Charles L. Dodgson [AKA Lewis Carroll].
Courtesy of Alexander D. Wainwright, Curator of the Morris L. Parrish Collection of Victorian Novelists, the Princeton University Library.

THE ROSES RACE
AROUND HER NAME
Poems from Fathers to Daughters

Edited by Jonathan Cott

STONEHILL

Book design by Ira Friedlander.

First printing, November, 1974.

ISBN: 088373-020-0

Printed in the United States of America

66738

CONTENTS

Preface
Introduction

PART I: Imaginary Daughters

PART II: Fathers to Daughters

PREFACE

The idea for *The Roses Race Around Her Name* occurred to me when I began to wonder why there were so many beautiful poems written by fathers to their daughters. For this anthology I have made what is obviously a "personal" selection, emphasizing, whenever I could, poems that directly address themselves to particular daughters (although not always the poets' own) and not just to girl children generally or to noble young ladies. For this reason, I have excluded many excellent odes and elegies to noble daughters by Jonson, Donne, and Dryden, as well as baby poems and album verses by poets such as Charles Lamb, Tennyson, and Walter de la Mare. And except for one long Chorus from Euripides' *Helen*, I have excluded dramatic writings; though it is easy to see how I might have included scores of selections from the Greek tragedies and Shakespeare, for example. Still, I hope I have included most of the major poems.

This anthology concentrates specifically on the father-daughter relationship; and for this reason I have obviously omitted poems by mothers to their daughters, since I believe that that relationship requires a special and different focus. In any event, it is certainly true that no relationship can be accurately and fully understood from just one perspective. And the converse view of the father-daughter world would be one that insisted on examining poems by daughters to their fathers.

Just as Athena, goddess of warriors, sprang full-born and self-willed out of the head of Zeus—"owl-eyed, inventive, unbending of heart, pure virgin, savior of cities, courageous, Tritogeneia"—so most of the well-known contemporary poems by daughters to their fathers (Sylvia Plath, Anne Sexton, Diane Wakoski, *et. al.*) reveal feelings of irreducible disappointment and bitterness—the "angel in the house" (in Virginia Woolf's words) coming home in anger to cry out, not so much against the fantasizing and projecting father as against the patriarchal and authoritarian regime represented and embodied by him. "In my next incarnation," Scottie Fitzgerald Lanahan writes about her father F. Scott Fitzgerald, "I may not choose again to be the daughter of a Famous Author. The pay is good, and there are fringe benefits, but the working conditions are too hazardous. . . . I was an imaginary daughter, as fictional as one of his early heroines."

I hope that someone will soon compile an anthology which presents the "other side" of the occasionally *ex parte* father-daughter relationship.

I would like to thank Annabel Levitt and Ira Friedlander who helped make this book possible.

On the deepest level, the nuclear family can be conceived of as a representation of an archetypal or algebraic matrix by which we attempt to explain and express our roots in nature, our endeavors and feelings, and even the origin and dissolution of cosmic occurrences. By means of familial relationships, we feel and think about the universes within and without. And it is in this sense that we can understand how "relationships" often represent permutations of a single "plot"—that of the family romance—and why, at the same time, we can learn to accept creation myths about the Children of the Sun or the explanation that the Dew is the daughter of the Moon and the Air.

In the more mundane realm of the nuclear family, every relationship (father-son, son-mother, mother-daughter, etc.) has its appropriate controlling image and myth. These images and myths that emblematize our feelings about each other are certainly determined, emphasized, and emotionally colored by varying social, cultural, and religious beliefs—e.g., Demeter and Persephone, Laius and Oedipus, Oedipus and Jocasta, Abraham and Isaac, the Virgin and Jesus, or Jesus and the Heavenly Father (a relationship hauntingly expressed in innumerable Bach chorales and in the Protestant tradition generally).

It might at first seem curious that in the realm of poetry it is specifically the father-daughter relationship that has occasioned such an extraordinary number of important and beautiful works. The reasons for this might seem surprising when we remember that in ancient and even fairly recent times, daughters were often considered expendable. In 1 B.C., Hilarion instructed his wife: "If, as may well happen, you give birth to a child, if it is a boy let it live; if it is a girl, expose it." Of six hundred families listed on second century inscriptions at Delphi, Jack Lindsay informs us in *The Ancient World*, only one per cent raised two daughters. It is only recently that daughters have been as uniformly desired as sons. Many contemporary women writers, of course, are pointing to the thousands of exceptions to this "acceptance" even today—as well as to the notorious lack of equality dispensed to grown-up daughters. "When we think of fathers and daughters," Elizabeth Fisher writes, "we think in double terms. There is the all-powerful father of the patriarchal hierarchy who owns his daughter and disposes of her to a husband, and there is the wished-for affectionate father of propinquity and growing up. The tradition of male despotism, absolute right within the family, still lingers, though much of the power has been eroded. For many of us, the missing father, the father who is feared and loved but remote and ungiving, still applies."

It must be said, however, that this idea of "equality" was not usually the motivating impulse underlying most poems written by fathers to either their daughters or their sons. In the not-so-proverbial olden days, young boys and girls were equally liable to the constraints of society. Consider Sir Walter Ralegh's unnerving warning to his child in his sonnet "To My Son," advising him to beware the coming together of "the wood, the weed, and the wag":

> Three things there be that prosper up apace
> And flourish, whilst they grow asunder far;
> But on a day, they meet all in one place,
> And when they meet, they one another mar.
> And they be these: the wood, the weed, the wag.
> The wood is that which makes the gallow tree;
> The weed is that which strings the hangman's
>   bag;
> The wag, my pretty knave, betokeneth thee.
> Mark well, dear boy, whilst these assemble not,
> Green springs the tree, hemp grows, the wag
>   is wild;
> But when they meet, it makes the timber rot,
> It frets the halter, and it chokes the child.
>   Then bless thee, and beware, and let us pray
>   We part not with thee at this meeting day.

Most poems to children from medieval to recent times have more gently but sanctimoniously exhorted and admonished their young listeners to keep a civil tongue, avoid covetousness, bow their knees, be meek and mild, and generally pretend that the swaddling bands were still strangling their limbs. Herrick's "My Daughter's Dowry" and, more tenderly, the seventeenth century "The Maiden's Best Adorning" both embody this attitude, as does John Lydgate's earlier but more oppressive "The Boy Serving at the Table":

> My dear child, first thyself enable
> With all thine heart to virtuous discipline;
> Afore thy sovereign, standing at the table,
> Dispose thou thee after my doctrine
> To all nurture thy courage to incline.
> First, when thou speakest be not reckless,
> Keep feet and fingers still in peace.
> Be simple of cheer, cast not thine eye aside,
> Gaze not about, turning thy sight over all.
> Against the post let not thy back abide,
> Neither make thy mirror of the wall.
> Pick not thy nose, and, most especial,
> Be well ware, and set hereon thy thought,
> Before thy sovereign scratch nor rub thee nought.

Nothing can better define the difference between the earlier and more recent attitudes towards children—male and female—than to contrast the above poems with a song like Bob Dylan's "Forever Young," which is itself a poem in this "teaching" tradition.

And for most poets today—in spite of the remaining vestiges of patriarchal hubris—the father-daughter relationship has certainly become a special area of empathic concern, for it is a relationship that, at least on the "creative" literary level, has been purified of conflict. "Away between the confusing world of forms," Lawrence Durrell writes of his sleeping child, for it is this quietude of sleep that allows the poet to imagine in reverie the possibility of an emollient and untroubled relationship.

Psychologically, we can begin to explain this lack of conflict by pointing paradigmatically to one of the medieval English Mystery Plays in which, on the first page, the Virgin Mary is talking to her infant son; yet, shortly thereafter—with the typical temporal compression characteristic of these plays—Jesus has been resurrected, Mary has become the daughter of God and is now talking as a child to her father—thereby resolving the incestuous paradox presented to us by Shakespeare in *Pericles*: "He's father, son, and husband mild / I mother, wife, and yet his child."* The inversion and transformational shift of the oedipal mother-son relationship reveals the relationship of the daughter to the father—and the sexual cathexis has been similarly inverted and neutralized. It is, however, often just this tension between affection and lust that haunts many of these poems—as it does many real life father-daughter relationships. But, significantly, the idealization inherent in the "radical innocence" both of the poetically perceived "daughter" and the father-daughter relationship itself has resulted in a number of poems to "imaginary" daughters, collected in Part 1 of this anthology. In this imagined world of ideal communication,† even Weldon Kees's bitter poem to a supposititious daughter simply reflects the obverse side of this world, just as it displays the obsessive sense of outraged innocence that we find in much of the work of this brilliant American poet who committed suicide in 1955.

---

* Think also of Dante's "O Virgin mother, daughter of thy son" (*Paradisio* XXXIII, 1).

† The reader might try to obtain Walter Lowenfels' wonderful book *To An Imaginary Daughter* (Horizon Press)—a part-diary / part-reverie / part-political meditation that concludes with the following entry: "It's 42 outside (5 a.m.) and that makes me think of you. Blizzards, stuck in the snow between there and here—and then, stuck here, without heat, no electricity, no road, nothing but snow. And it hasn't passed yet. It is *en route* again, in that bean-shaped route that time and the solar system take, according to what I am reading about the Von Weizsacker theory

It is specifically in the realm of the imagination that fathers often discover their daughters, and it sometimes seems to be the case that the image of the daughter immediately and to an astonishing degree suggests the nature of the poetic process itself. In *Don du Poème* (Gift of the Poem), the French poet Mallarmé hints at a connection between the conceiving and writing of a poem and the giving birth to a daughter:

Idumean night child pressing from my womb:
Dark, with bleeding wing and pale, the plume
Plucked, through the glass burned deep with spice
    and gold,
Through iced white panes, dreary, alas, still cold,
Dawn forced itself on the angelic lamp,
O palms! and when it showed this relic's stamp
To father, trying on a chilling smile,
Blue-barren solitude quailed like a child.
With daughter, nurse, and with the innocence
Of icy feet, welcome a birth of anguish:
Voice recalling viol and harpsichord,
Will you, with withered finger, now adore
The breast where woman flows in sibyl white
For lips that itch from air's blue virgin sky?

(my translation)

In "A Prayer for My Daughter," W. B. Yeats desired his child to be "like some green laurel / Rooted in one dear perpetual place." And one begins to realize that Yeats's notion of "radical innocence" suggested a life coterminous

---

of the origin of the universe. Just one ice age after another, with tiny breaths in between—frosty bits of fog during which there was human breath once upon a time, between the cycles of no return. So your being here was in tune with infinite processes. And your spirit will feel at home in the great beyond as the stellar dust keeps on congealing and tightening and loosening. And other Winifreds in other worlds will also freeze their hair and laugh between breaths as the helium and hydrogen fight it out for survival. At last I feel sorry for them, which is more than they can feel about us, for they will never know what they missed not being here the day Winifred got stuck in a blizzard 13 star centuries south of the Little Dipper, Weymouth, N.J."

with the poet's ideal of the "Image," the incarnation of which is the dancer who "outdanced thought—intellect and emotion . . . for the moment one"—a state the poet allotted to the gyre of Phase 15 in his metaphysic. Simply, his daughter was to be the poet's image of Art. And, conversely, it is interesting to note that poets' ideas of their own artistic dimensions often suggest the values they deem it proper to wish upon and admire in a child. In "Born Yesterday," for example, the English poet Philip Larkin writes:

> May you be ordinary;
> Have, like other women,
> An average of talents:
> Not ugly, not good-looking,
> Nothing uncustomary
> To pull you off your balance,
> That, unworkable itself,
> Stops all the rest from working.
> In fact, may you be dull—
> If that is what a skilled,
> Vigilant, flexible,
> Unemphasised, enthralled
> Catching of happiness is called.

The poet is, of course, defining exactly his own poetic style.

In "The Lost Children," Randall Jarrell makes an acute connection between the birth and the gradual coming-of-independence of a child and the artist's possession and inevitable loss of "control" over his own creation. In the guise of a mother of two little girls—one, or possibly both, imaginary—the poet writes:

> It is strange
> To carry inside you someone else's body;
> To know it before it's born;
> To see at last that it's a boy or girl, and perfect;
> To bathe it and dress it; to watch it
> Nurse at your breast, till you almost know it
> Better than you know yourself—better than it
>   knows itself.

You own it as you made it.
You are the authority upon it.

But as the child learns
To take care of herself, you know her less.
Her accidents, adventures are her own,
You lose track of them. Still, you know more
About her than anyone *except* her.

Little by little the child in her dies.
You say, "I have lost a child, but gained a
    friend."
You feel yourself gradually discarded.
She argues with you or ignores you
Or is kind to you. She who begged to follow you
Anywhere, just so long as it was you,
Finds follow the leader no more fun.
She makes few demands; you are grateful for the
    few.

In this lucid and accurate observation of the Poem as
Child, the daughter finally becomes "the authority upon
herself"—the New Critical Poem itself: a complex image,
autotelic with coincident form and meaning! Yet it is also a
poem that is now given to the world, no longer belonging
to the poet alone.

It is this "self-begotten" child who resists becoming the
poet's Galatea, an appanage of his fantasies, though the
poet will continue to try to have his way. But it is this
perception of the daughter as "self-delighting, self-appeasing, self-affrighting" (Yeats) and "small, contained, and
fragile" (Yvor Winters) that forces the poet to accept the
ideas of distance and of loss. "The round gaze of her
childhood was / White as the distance in the glass / Or on a
white page," Stephen Spender writes. And it is in this
glass, this mirror, that the poet sees himself, his fantasies,
his premonitions of old age and solitude; and it is on his
white page that he must write of these.

"I sleep so that in the silence / I can more clearly understand / myself," David Ignatow addresses his daughter:
"We are here to make each other die / with perfect willing-

ness." "Don't grow old, don't die," Galway Kinnell's daughter says to the flower in "Little Sleep's-Head." But she is also talking to her father, just as he is talking to her and to himself about the "still undanced cadence of vanishing."

"Man is in love and loves what vanishes," Yeats writes. And the image of the daughter—Joyce's "rosefrail and fair ... blueveined child"—suggests transparency, dissolution, and disappearance. It is not well known that Thomas de Quincey went into a long period of derangement on the death of Wordsworth's four-year-old daughter, Catherine, in 1812 (see the Wordsworth poems in this collection). In remembering this little girl, De Quincey (foreshadowing the nympholeptic grief of Nabokov's Humbert Humbert) writes:

> Over and above my excess love for her, I had always viewed her as an impersonation of the dawn and the spirit of infancy; and this abstraction seated in her person, together with the visionary sort of connexion which, even in her parting hours, she assumed with the summer sun, by timing her immersion into the cloud of death with the rising and setting of that fountain of life—these combined impressions recoiled so violently into a contrast or polar antithesis to the image of death that each exalted and brightened the other.

In his frenzy, De Quincey hallucinated Catherine in the fields:

> Almost always she carried a basket on her head; and usually the first hint upon which the figure arose commenced in wild plants, such as tall ferns, or the purple flowers of the foxglove; but, whatever might be the colours or the forms, uniformly the same little full-formed figure arose, uniformly dressed in the little blue bedgown and black skirt of Westmoreland, and uniformly with the air of advancing motion.

And it is a similar loss that leads the fourteenth century *Pearl* poet to fall grief-stricken on the mound where he has lost his "pearl"—his angelic child—only to fall into a trance-like dream during which he recognizes his child, now transfigured and joined in Eternal Spousal as bride to the Lamb, one of the company of the 144,000, untainted by spot or blemish, seen by John in the Apocalyptic vision of the New Jerusalem.

But in the quieter regions of the heart—beyond transfiguration and projection—the poems in this anthology continually remind us of the possibilities of the unassailable integrity in the encounter of two human beings subsisting in a consubstantial relationship of acceptance, sympathy, and devotion: Kenneth Rexroth's mountain journey with his young companion, W.D. Snodgrass visiting the zoo with his child, and David Ignatow replying to his daughter's question with words belied by the truths of the world but true to the world of the heart:

We're not going to die,
We'll find a way.
We'll breathe deeply
and eat carefully.
We'll think always on life.
There'll be no fading for you or for me.
We'll be the first
and we'll not laugh at ourselves ever
and your children will be my grandchildren.
Nothing will have changed
except by addition.
There'll never be another as you
and never another as I.
No one ever will confuse you
nor confuse me with another.
We will not be forgotten and passed over
and buried under the births and deaths to come.

Jonathan Cott
New York City

PART I

IMAGINARY DAUGHTERS

Still she haunts me, phantomwise.
Alice moving under skies
Never seen by waking eyes.

Lewis Carroll

Theodore Roethke

ELEGY FOR JANE
(My Student, Thrown by a Horse)

I remember the neckcurls, limp and damp as tendrils;
And her quick look, a sidelong pickerel smile;
And how, once startled into talk, the light syllables leaped for
    her,
And she balanced in the delight of her thought,
A wren, happy, tail into the wind,
Her song trembling the twigs and small branches.
The shade sang with her;
The leaves, their whispers turned to kissing;
And the mould sang in the bleached valleys under the rose.

Oh, when she was sad, she cast herself down into such a pure
    depth,
Even a father could not find her:
Scraping her cheek against straw;
Stirring the clearest water.

My sparrow, you are not here,
Waiting like a fern, making a spiney shadow.
The sides of wet stones cannot console me,
Nor the moss, wound with the last light.

If only I could nudge you from this sleep,
My maimed darling, my skittery pigeon.
Over this damp grave I speak the words of my love:
I, with no rights in this matter,
Neither father nor lover.

4

Weldon Kees

FOR MY DAUGHTER

Looking into my daughter's eyes I read
Beneath the innocence of morning flesh
Concealed, hintings of death she does not heed.
Coldest of winds have blown this hair, and mesh
Of seaweed snarled these miniatures of hands;
The night's slow poison, tolerant and bland,
Has moved her blood. Parched years that I have seen
That may be hers appear: foul, lingering
Death in certain war, the slim legs green.
Or, fed on hate, she relishes the sting
Of others' agony; perhaps the cruel
Bride of a syphilitic or a fool.
These speculations sour in the sun.
I have no daughters. I desire none.

John Ashbery

THOUGHTS OF A YOUNG GIRL

"It is such a beautiful day I had to write you a letter
From the tower, and to show I'm not mad:
I only slipped on the cake of soap of the air
And drowned in the bathtub of the world.
You were too good to cry much over me.
And now I let you go. Signed, The Dwarf."

I passed by late in the afternoon
And the smile still played about her lips
As it has for centuries. She always knows
How to be utterly delightful. Oh my daughter,
My sweetheart, daughter of my late employer, princess,
May you not be long on the way!

William Carlos Williams

YOUTH AND BEAUTY

I bought a dishmop—
having no daughter—
for they had twisted
fine ribbons of shining copper
about white twine
and made a tousled head
of it, fastened it
upon a turned ash stick
slender at the neck
straight, tall—
when tied upright
on the brass wallbracket
to be a light for me
and naked
as a girl should seem
to her father.

Jonathan Cott

HE SPENDS TIME IN SOUTHERN CALIFORNIA

I could ride the Disneyland sky ride forever.
It is always tea time or perpetual autumn,
my Duino, fireworks above my head.
The poets' girl friends ride the bobsled—Maud, Milena . . .
Fenimore sits alone.
I see them all blondes, flighty pink ribbons,
threes in their convertibles zooming home.

Down south, a love note on my door:
"Your intellectuality is so strong it destroys my womanhood"
or "Your mouth renders me mad."
Instead, they open up the surf with their dizzy teeth,
thousands of sprinklers light rainbows on the lawn,
even poison pink oleander trees make me cling.

They come again and stay.
In twenty years they look up, mild with pleasure,
and in fifty, too, back like the sea,
back with their careless limbs.
They are always coming to me like Friedrich's
great beautiful cats of prey.
How they leave me with their wrists,
yet I fly above it.

In my heart of daughters they look lovelier than wild peacock
    feathers,
shoots under moss, arms, stems. . . .
They come to the breathing names, watering the brush:
Borrego Springs, Mesa Grande, Escondido, Solana Beach,
and there is always a happy day,
and now you abandon me.

Randall Jarrell

THE LOST CHILDREN

Two little girls, one fair, one dark,
One alive, one dead, are running hand in hand
Through a sunny house. The two are dressed
In red and white gingham, with puffed sleeves and sashes.
They run away from me . . . But I am happy;
When I wake I feel no sadness, only delight.
I've seen them again, and I am comforted
That, somewhere, they still are.

It is strange
To carry inside you someone else's body;
To know it before it's born;
To see at last that it's a boy or girl, and perfect;
To bathe it and dress it; to watch it
Nurse at your breast, till you almost know it
Better than you know yourself—better than it knows itself.
You own it as you made it.
You are the authority upon it.

But as the child learns
To take care of herself, you know her less.
Her accidents, adventures are her own,
You lose track of them. Still, you know more
About her than anyone *except* her.

Little by little the child in her dies.
You say, "I have lost a child, but gained a friend."
You feel yourself gradually discarded.
She argues with you or ignores you
Or is kind to you. She who begged to follow you
Anywhere, just so long as it was you,
Finds follow the leader no more fun.
She makes few demands; you are grateful for the few.

The young person who writes once a week
Is the authority upon herself.
She sits in my living room and shows her husband
My albums of her as a child. He enjoys them
And makes fun of them. I look too
And I realize the girl in the matching blue
Mother-and-daughter dress, the fair one carrying
The tin lunch box with the half-pint thermos bottle
Or training her pet duck to go down the slide
Is lost just as the dark one, who is dead, is lost.
But the world in which the two wear their flared coats
And the hats that match, exists so uncannily
That, after I've seen its pictures for an hour,
I believe in it: the bandage coming loose
One has in the picture of the other's birthday,
The castles they are building, at the beach for asthma.
I look at them and all the old sure knowledge
Floods over me, when I put the album down
I keep saying inside: "I *did* know those children.
I braided those braids. I was driving the car
The day that she stepped in the can of grease
We were taking to the butcher for our ration points.
I *know* those children. I know all about them.
Where are they?"

I stare at her and try to see some sign
Of the child she was. I can't believe there isn't any.
I tell her foolishly, pointing at the picture,
That I keep wondering where she is.
She tells me, "Here I am."
                                    Yes, and the other
Isn't dead, but has everlasting life . . .

The girl next door, the borrowed child,
Said to me the other day, "You like children so much,
Don't you want to have some of your own?"
I couldn't believe that she could say it.
I thought: "Surely you can look at me and see them."

When I see them in my dreams I feel such joy.
If I could dream of them every night!

When I think of my dream of the little girls
It's as if we were playing hide-and-seek.
The dark one
Looks at me longingly, and disappears;
The fair one stays in sight, just out of reach
No matter where I reach. I am tired
As a mother who's played all day, some rainy day.
I don't want to play any more, I don't want to,
But the child keeps on playing, so I play.

PART II

POEMS TO DAUGHTERS

Carry me along, taddy, like you done through
the toy fair.

James Joyce

Kenneth Rexroth

THE WHEEL REVOLVES

You were a girl of satin and gauze
Now you are my mountain and waterfall companion.
Long ago I read those lines of Po Chu I
Written in his middle age.
Young as I was they touched me.
I never thought in my own middle age
I would have a beautiful young dancer
To wander with me by falling crystal waters,
Among mountains of snow and granite,
Least of all that unlike Po's girl
She would be my very daughter.

The earth turns toward the sun.
Summer comes to the mountains.
Blue grouse drum in the red fir woods
All the bright long days.
You put blue jay and flicker feathers
In your hair.
Two and two violet green swallows
Play over the lake.
The blue birds have come back
To nest on the little island.
The swallows sip water on the wing
And play at love and dodge and swoop
Just like the swallows that swirl
Under and over the Ponte Vecchio.
Light rain crosses the lake
Hissing faintly. After the rain
There are giant puffballs with tortoise shell backs
At the edge of the meadow.
Snows of a thousand winters
Melt in the sun of one summer.
Wild cyclamen bloom by the stream.
Trout veer in the transparent current.

In the evening marmots bark in the rocks.
The Scorpion curls over the glimmering ice field.
A white crowned night sparrow sings as the moon sets.
Thunder growls far off.
Our campfire is a single light
Amongst a hundred peaks and waterfalls.
The manifold voices of falling water
Talk all night.
Wrapped in your down bag
Starlight on your cheeks and eyelids
Your breath comes and goes
In a tiny cloud in the frosty night.
Ten thousand birds sing in the sunrise.
Ten thousand years revolve without change.
All this will never be again.

John Skelton

To MISTRESS ISABEL PENNELL

By Saint Mary, my lady,
Your mammy and your daddy
Brought forth a goodly baby!

My maiden Isabel,
Reflaring rosabel.
The fragrant camomel;
  The rudy rosary,
The sovereign rosemary,
The pretty strawberry;
  The columbine, the nept,
The jelofer well set,
The proper violet:
Ennewéd your colour
Is like the daisy flower
After the April shower;
  Star of the morrow gray,
The blossom on the spray,
The freshest flower of May;
  Maidenly demure,
Of womanhood the lure;
Wherefore I make you sure

It were an heavenly health,
It were an endless wealth,
A life for God himself,
  To hear this nightingale
Among the birdes smale
Warbeling in the vale,
    Dug, dug,
    Jug, jug,
      Good year and good luck,
      With chuck, chuck, chuck, chuck!

16

William Blake

THE LITTLE GIRL LOST

In futurity
I prophetic see
That the earth from sleep
(Grave the sentence deep)

Shall arise and seek
For her maker meek;
And the desart wild
Become a garden mild.

In the southern clime,
Where the summer's prime
Never fades away,
Lovely Lyca lay.

Seven summers old
Lovely Lyca told;
She had wander'd long
Hearing wild birds' song.

"Sweet sleep, come to me
"Underneath this tree.
"Do father, mother weep,
"Where can Lyca sleep?

"Lost in desart wild
"Is your little child.
"How can Lyca sleep
"If her mother weep?

"If her heart does ake
"Then let Lyca wake;
"If my mother sleep,
"Lyca shall not weep.

"Frowning, frowning night,
"O'er this desart bright
"Let thy moon arise
"While I close my eyes."

Sleeping Lyca lay
While the beasts of prey,
Come from caverns deep,
View'd the maid asleep.

The kingly lion stood
And the virgin view'd,
Then he gambol'd round
O'er the hallow'd ground.

Leopards, tygers, play
Round her as she lay,
While the lion old
Bow'd his mane of gold

And her bosom lick,
And upon her neck
From his eyes of flame
Ruby tears there came;

While the lioness
Loos'd her slender dress,
And naked they convey'd
To caves the sleeping maid.

William Blake

THE LITTLE GIRL FOUND

All the night in woe
Lyca's parents go
Over vallies deep,
While the desarts weep.

Tired and woe-begone,
Hoarse with making moan,
Arm in arm seven days
They trac'd the desart ways.

Seven nights they sleep
Among shadows deep,
And dream they see their child
Starv'd in desart wild.

Pale, thro' pathless ways
The fancied image strays
Famish'd, weeping, weak,
With hollow piteous shriek.

Rising from unrest,
The trembling woman prest
With feet of weary woe:
She could no further go.

In his arms he bore
Her, arm'd with sorrow sore;
Till before their way
A couching lion lay.

Turning back was vain:
Soon his heavy mane
Bore them to the ground.
Then he stalk'd around,

Smelling to his prey;
But their fears allay
When he licks their hands,
And silent by them stands.

They look upon his eyes
Fill'd with deep surprise,
And wondering behold
A Spirit arm'd in gold.

On his head a crown,
On his shoulders down
Flow'd his golden hair.
Gone was all their care.

"Follow me," he said;
"Weep not for the maid;
"In my palace deep
"Lyca lies asleep."

Then they followed
Where the vision led,
And saw their sleeping child
Among tygers wild.

To this day they dwell
In a lonely dell;
Nor fear the wolvish howl
Nor the lion's growl.

Euripides

CHORUS FROM *HELEN*
Translated by Richmond Lattimore

Long ago, the Mountain Mother
of all the gods, on flashing feet,
ran down the wooded clefts
of the hills, crossed stream-waters in spate
and the sea's thunderous surf beat
in wild desire for the lost girl
not to be named, her daughter,
and the cry of her voice keened high to break
through mutter of drums and rattles.
And as the goddess harnessed
wild beasts to draw her chariot
in search of the daughter torn away
from the circling pattern of dance where she
and her maidens moved, storm-footed beside
the mother, Artemis with her bow,
stark eyed, spear-handed Athene
attended. But Zeus, from his high place
in the upper sky shining ordained
a different course to follow.

For when the wandering and the swift
course of the mother was done, the far,
the toilsome, the vain search
for her daughter's treacherous capture,
she crossed the place where the mountain nymphs
keep watch in the snows of Ida,
and there cast the blight of her grief
across the stone and snow of the hill forests.
Earth, green gone from her fields, would give
food no more in the sown lands,
and generations were wasted.
For the flocks she shot out no longer
tender food from the curling leaves.

The cities of men were starving,
the sacrifice to the gods was gone,
no offerings flamed on the altars. She,
turned cruel by grief for her daughter, dried
the springs that gush from deep in the ground,
and there were no jets of bright water.

But now, as those festivals the gods
share with the race of men died out,
Zeus spoke, to soften the ruinous
rages of the Great Mother:
"Go, stately Graces, and go
Muses, to Deio angered
thus for the sake of the maiden.
Change with wild singing the strain of grief
in her, and with choral and dancing."
It was then that the loveliest
of the immortals took the death—
voice of bronze and the skin-strung drums:
Aphrodite. The goddess smiled
and drew into her hands
the deep sounding flute
in delight with its music.

You had no right in this. The flames you lit
in your chambers were without sanction.
You showed, child, no due reverence
for this goddess' sacrifice.
You won the great mother's anger.
The dappled dress in the deer skin
is a great matter, and the ivy wound
green on the sacred hollow reed
has power; so also the shaken,
the high, the whirled course of the wheel
in the air; so also the dances,
the wild hair shaken for Bromius,
the goddess' nightlong vigils.
It is well that by daylight
the moon obscures her.
All your claim was your beauty.

William Butler Yeats

A PRAYER FOR MY DAUGHTER

Once more the storm is howling, and half hid
Under this cradle-hood and coverlid
My child sleeps on. There is no obstacle
But Gregory's wood and one bare hill
Whereby the haystack- and roof-levelling wind,
Bred on the Atlantic, can be stayed;
And for an hour I have walked and prayed
Because of the great gloom that is in my mind.

I have walked and prayed for this young child an hour
And heard the sea-wind scream upon the tower,
And under the arches of the bridge, and scream
In the elms above the flooded stream;
Imagining in excited reverie
That the future years had come,
Dancing to a frenzied drum,
Out of the murderous innocence of the sea.

May she be granted beauty and yet not
Beauty to make a stranger's eye distraught,
Or hers before a looking-glass, for such,
Being made beautiful overmuch,
Consider beauty a sufficient end,
Lose natural kindness and maybe
The heart-revealing intimacy
That chooses right, and never find a friend.

Helen being chosen found life flat and dull
And later had much trouble from a fool,
While that great Queen, that rose out of the spray,
Being fatherless could have her way
Yet chose a bandy-leggèd smith for man.
It's certain that fine women eat
A crazy salad with their meat
Whereby the Horn of Plenty is undone.

In courtesy I'd have her chiefly learned;
Hearts are not had as a gift but hearts are earned
By those that are not entirely beautiful;
Yet many, that have played the fool
For beauty's very self, has charm made wise,
And many a poor man that has roved,
Loved and thought himself beloved,
From a glad kindness cannot take his eyes.

May she become a flourishing hidden tree
That all her thoughts may like the linnet be,
And have no business but dispensing round
Their magnanimities of sound,
Nor but in merriment begin a chase,
Nor but in merriment a quarrel.
O may she live like some green laurel
Rooted in one dear perpetual place.

My mind, because the minds that I have loved,
The sort of beauty that I have approved,
Prosper but little, has dried up of late,
Yet knows that to be choked with hate
May well be of all evil chances chief.
If there's no hatred in a mind
Assault and battery of the wind
Can never tear the linnet from the leaf.

An intellectual hatred is the worst,
So let her think opinions are accursed.
Have I not seen the loveliest women born
Out of the mouth of Plenty's horn,
Because of her opinionated mind
Barter that horn and every good
By quiet natures understood
For an old bellows full of angry wind?

Considering that, all hatred driven hence,
The soul recovers radical innocence
And learns at last that it is self-delighting,

Self-appeasing, self-affrighting,
And that its own sweet will is Heaven's will;
She can, though every face should scowl
And every windy quarter howl
Or every bellows burst, be happy still.

And may her bridegroom bring her to a house
Where all's accustomed, ceremonious;
For arrogance and hatred are the wares
Peddled in the thoroughfares.
How but in custom and in ceremony
Are innocence and beauty born?
Ceremony's a name for the rich horn,
And custom for the spreading laurel tree.

Robert Burns

A POET'S WELCOME TO HIS LOVE-BEGOTTEN DAUGHTER

I

Thou's welcome, wean! Mishanter fa' me,   MISHAP
If thoughts o' thee or yet thy mammie
Shall ever daunton me or awe me,
     My sweet, wee lady,
Or if I blush when thou shalt ca' me
     Tyta or daddie!

II

What tho' they ca' me fornicator,
An' tease my name in kintra clatter?   COUNTRY GOSSIP
The mair they talk, I'm kend the better;   KNOWN
     E'en let them clash!
An auld wife's tongue's a feckless matter
     To gie ane fash.   GIVE, BOTHER

III

Welcome, my bonie, sweet, wee dochter!
Tho' ye come here a wee unsought for,
And tho' your comin I hae fought for
     Baith kirk and queir;   CHURCH, CHOIR
Yet, by my faith, ye're no unwrought for—
     That I shall swear!

The "wean" of this Address—subtitled "The First Instance That En-·
titled Him to the Venerable Appellation of Father"—was the poet's
daughter Elizabeth, by Elizabeth Paton, a servant at Lochlie. The child
was born in November, 1784 and was brought by the father to Mossgiel.
She was later raised by Burns's mother and brother.

IV

Sweet fruit o' monie a merry dint,   MANY
My funny toil is no a' tint: ALL LOST
Tho' thou cam to the warl' asklent,   ASKEW
      Which fools may scoff at,
In my last plack thy part's be in't   WILL, SHARE SHALL BE
      The better half o't.

V

Tho' I should be the waur bestead,   WORSE CIRCUMSTANCED
Thou's be as braw and bienly clad,   FINE, WARMLY
And thy young years as nicely bred
      Wi' education,
As onie brat o' wedlock's bed
      In a' thy station.

VI

Wee image o' my bonie Betty,
As fatherly I kiss and daut thee,   FONDLE
As dear and near my heart I set thee,
      Wi' as guid will,
As a' the priests had seen me get thee
      That's out o' Hell.

VIII

Gude grant that thou may ay inherit
Thy mither's looks an' gracefu' merit,
An' thy poor, worthless daddie's spirit
      Without his failins!
'T will please me mair to see thee heir it
      Than stocket mailins.   SMALL-HOLDINGS

VIII

And if thou be what I wad hae thee,
An' tak the counsel I shall gie thee,
I'll never rue my trouble wi' thee—
      The cost nor shame o't—
But be a loving father to thee,
      And brag the name o't.

John Crowe Ransom

BELLS FOR JOHN WHITESIDE'S DAUGHTER

There was such speed in her little body,
And such lightness in her footfall,
It is no wonder her brown study
Astonishes us all.

Her wars were bruited in our high window.
We looked among orchard trees and beyond
Where she took arms against her shadow,
Or harried unto the pond.

The lazy geese, like a snow cloud
Dripping their snow on the green grass,
Tricking and stopping, sleepy and proud,
Who cried in goose, Alas,

For the tireless heart within the little
Lady with rod that made them rise
From their noon apple-dreams and scuttle
Goose-fashion under the skies!

But now go the bells, and we are ready,
In one house we are sternly stopped
To say we are vexed at her brown study,
Lying so primly propped.

Philip Larkin

BORN YESTERDAY
For Sally Amis

Tightly-folded bud,
I have wished you something
None of the others would:
Not the usual stuff
About being beautiful,
Or running off a spring
Of innocence and love—
They will all wish you that,
And should it prove possible,
Well, you're a lucky girl.

But if it shouldn't, then
May you be ordinary;
Have, like other women,
An average of talents:
Not ugly, not good-looking,
Nothing uncustomary
To pull you off your balance,
That, unworkable itself,
Stops all the rest from working.
In fact, may you be dull—
If that is what a skilled,
Vigilant, flexible,
Unemphasized, enthralled
Catching of happiness is called.

Richard Wilbur

FOR ELLEN

On eyes embarked for sleep the only light
Goes off, and there is nothing that you know
So well, it may not monster in this sea.
The vine leaves pat the screen. Viciously free,
The wind vaults over the roof with Mister Crow
To drop his crooked laughter in your night.

And morning's cannonades of brightness come
To a little utter blueness in your eyes.
You stagger goldenly, bestowing blue;
Blue heal-all breaks the pavingstone where you
Expect it, and you laugh in pure surprise
At the comic cripple hurdling to his slum.

But sometime you will look at the lazy sun
Hammocked in clouds, dead-slumbering in the sky.
That casual fire will blister blue, and night
Will strand its fears; then with a starker sight
And newer darker love, you will supply
The world of joy which never was begun.

William Stafford

THINKING FOR BERKY

In the late night listening from bed
I have joined the ambulance or the patrol
screaming toward some drama, the kind of end
that Berky must have some day, if she isn't dead.
The wildest of all, her father and mother cruel,
farming out there beyond the old stone quarry
where highschool lovers parked their lurching cars,
Berky learned to love in that dark school.

Early her face was turned away from home
toward any hardworking place; but still her soul,
with terrible things to do, was alive, looking out
for the rescue that—surely, some day—would have to come.

Windiest nights, Berky, I have thought for you,
and no matter how lucky I've been I've touched wood.
There are things not solved in our town though tomorrow
    came:
there are things time passing can never make come true.

We live in an occupied country, misunderstood;
justice will take us millions of intricate moves.
Sirens will hunt down Berky, you survivors in your beds
listening through the night, so far and good.

Walter Lowenfels

FOR MY DAUGHTER'S 20TH BIRTHDAY

You looked at me today
 with such pity for my age,
I felt sorry for something—
 I forget which.
 My beautiful stranger,
let's face it—you
 also are not the angel head
you came with twenty years ago.

What bothers me, my darling, is not age
 but the aged.
To get a breath of fresh air
 away from my generation
I visited my ancestors yesterday—
 the dinosaurs
 on the fourth floor of the museum.
I love the uselessness of these 100-foot memories;
they have nothing to say to me
 and they have not been saying it
 for eighty million years.

> *Pity the poor*
> *dinosaur*
> *He doesn't live here*
> *any more.*

What a relief to be able to visit
 the age group under us!
(Consider the traffic jam
 if death didn't help rid us
 of these monsters—our dead selves.)

 For my was-ness
I have no excuse—

just an old buffalo head
lifting my snout on the crowded prairie
   of my generation;
not even suggesting that we hurry along
   or be anything other than we are.
I can cure everything but my age—a disease
   which follows me to the grave—
after which I convalesce.

Matthew Prior

TO A CHILD OF QUALITY FIVE YEARS OLD

Lords, knights, and squires, the numerous band
   That wear the fair Miss Mary's fetters,
Were summoned by her high command,
   To show their passions by their letters.

My pen amongst the rest I took,
   Lest those bright eyes that cannot read
Should dart their kindling fires, and look
   The power they have to be obeyed.

Nor quality nor reputation
   Forbid me yet my flame to tell;
Dear Five-years-old befriends my passion,
   And I may write till she can spell.

For while she makes her silkworms beds
   With all the tender things I swear,
Whilst all the house my passion reads,
   In papers round her baby's hair,

She may receive and own my flame,
   For though the strictest prudes should know it,
She'll pass for a most virtuous dame,
   And I for an unhappy poet.

Then too, alas! when she shall tear
   The lines some younger rival sends,
She'll give me leave to write, I fear,
   And we shall still continue friends;

For, as our different ages move,
   'Tis so ordained, would fate but mend it,
That I shall be past making love
   When she begins to comprehend it.

The Child of Quality is Lady Mary Villiers (c. 1690–1735), daughter of
the first Earl of Jersey. In 1700 Prior was praising Mary's ability to
write.

Chuck Berry

MEMPHIS, TENNESSEE

Long distance information, get me Memphis, Tennessee,
Help me find the party trying to get in touch with me.
She could not leave her number, but I know who placed the
　call,
Cause my uncle took the message and he wrote it on the wall.

Help me information, get in touch with my Marie,
She's the only one who'd phone me here from Memphis,
　Tennessee.
Her home is on the south side, high up on a ridge,
Just a half a mile from the Mississippi Bridge.

Help me information, more than that I cannot add,
Only that I miss her and all the fun we had.
But we were pulled apart because her Mom did not agree,
And tore apart our happy home in Memphis, Tennessee.

Last time I saw Marie, she's waving me goodbye,
With hurry home drops on her cheek that trickled from her
　eye,
Marie is only six years old, information please,
Try to put me through to her in Memphis, Tennessee.

Archilochos

ON THE DAUGHTER OF LYKAMBES

O might
I but touch
Neobule's hand

The extant works of Archilochos, the seventh century B.C. mercenary soldier and poet, consist of not much more than three hundred extraordinary fragments, paraphrases, and indirect quotations. The poet was contracted to marry Neobule, a daughter of Lykambes, but when her father cancelled the wedding, Archilochos wrote a series of vindictive poems against Lykambes. Praised by Meleager as "a thistle with graceful leaves," Archilochos is the creator of some of the most passionate verse ever written, verse which today seems even more intense and contemporaneous in its existing fragmented form. (See *The Fragments of Archilochos* in the sharp, radiant translation by Guy Davenport.) The rendering of "On the Daughter of Lykambes" is by the editor.

Andrew Marvell

YOUNG LOVE

Come little infant, love me now,
  While thine unsuspected years
Clear thine agëd father's brow
  From cold jealousy and fears.

Pretty surely 'twere to see
  By young love old time beguiled:
While our sportings are as free
  As the nurse's with the child.

Common beauties stay fifteen;
  Such as yours should swifter move;
Whose fair blossoms are too green
  Yet for lust, but not for love.

Love as much the snowy lamb
  Or the wanton kid does prize,
As the lusty bull or ram,
  For his morning sacrifice.

Now then love me: time may take
  Thee before thy time away:
Of this need we'll virtue make,
  And learn love before we may.

So we win of doubtful fate;
  And, if good she to us meant,
We that good shall antedate;
  Or, if ill, that ill prevent.

Thus as kingdoms, frustrating
  Other titles to their crown,
In the cradle crown their king,
  So all foreign claims to drown;

So, to make all rivals vain,
  Now I crown thee with my love:
Crown me with thy love again,
  And we both shall monarchs prove.

Vladimir Nabokov

WANTED, WANTED: DOLORES HAZE

Wanted, wanted: Dolores Haze.
Hair: brown. Lips: scarlet.
Age: five thousand three hundred days.
Profession: none, or "starlet."

Where are you hiding, Dolores Haze?
Why are you hiding, darling?
(I talk in a daze, I walk in a maze,
I cannot get out, said the starling).

Where are you riding, Dolores Haze?
What make is the magic carpet?
Is a Cream Cougar the present craze?
And where are you parked, my car pet?

Who is your hero, Dolores Haze?
Still one of those blue-caped star-men?
Oh the balmy days and the palmy bays,
And the cars, and the bars, my Carmen!

Oh Dolores, that juke-box hurts!
Are you still dancin', darlin'?
(Both in worn levis, both in torn T-shirts,
And I, in my corner, snarlin').

Happy, happy is gnarled McFate
Touring the States with a child wife,
Plowing his Molly in every State
Among the protected wild life.

From *Lolita*. This is Humbert Humbert's poem for his vanished step-
daughter Dolores (Lolita) Haze.

My Dolly, my folly! Her eyes were *vair*,
And never closed when I kissed her.
Know an old perfume called *Soleil Vert*?
Are you from Paris, mister?

L'autre soir un air froid d'opéra m'alita;
Son félé—bien fol est qui s'y fie!
Il neige, le décor s'écroule, Lolita!
Lolita, qu'ai-je fait de ta vie?

Dying, dying, Lolita Haze,
Of hate and remorse, I'm dying.
And again my hairy fist I raise,
And again I hear you crying.

Officer, officer, there they go—
In the rain, where that lighted store is!
And her socks are white, and I love her so,
And her name is Haze, Dolores.

Officer, officer, there they are—
Dolores Haze and her lover!
Whip out your gun and follow that car.
Now tumble out, and take cover.

Wanted, wanted: Dolores Haze.
Her dream-gray gaze never flinches.
Ninety pounds is all she weighs
With a height of sixty inches.

My car is limping, Dolores Haze,
And the last long lap is the hardest,
And I shall be dumped where the weed decays,
And the rest is rust and stardust.

Quechua Song

WHEN YOU FIND YOURSELF ALONE
Translated by J.M. Arguedas and Ruth Stephan

When you find yourself alone on the river island
your father will not be there to call to you
alau, my daughter!
your mother cannot reach you there with
alau, my daughter!

The royal drake alone is there to walk at night with you
with the rain in his eyes,
with his tears of blood,
the rain in his eyes
tears of blood.

And the royal drake, even, must go away
when the waves of the river
become strong,
when the waves of the river
rush headlong.

But then I will go to walk at night with you,
singing:
I will rob you of your young heart on the island,
your young heart
I must steal.

This song was translated from Quechua into Spanish by J.M. Arguedas
and into English by Ruth Stephan.

James Joyce

Passage from FINNEGANS WAKE

night by silentsailing night white infantina Isobel (who will
be blushing all day to be, when she growed up one Sunday, Saint
Holy and Saint Ivory, when she took the veil, the beautiful
presentation nun, so barely twenty, in her pure coif, sister
Isobel, and next Sunday, Mistlemas, when she looked a peach,
the beautiful Samaritan, still as beautiful and still in her teens,
nurse Saintette Isabelle, with stiffstarched cuffs but on Holiday,
Christmas, Easter mornings when she wore a wreath, the
wonderful widow of eighteen springs, Madame Isa Veuve La
Belle, so sad but lucksome in her boyblue's long black with
orange blossoming weeper's veil) for she was the only girl they
loved, as she is the queenly pearl you prize, because of the way
the night that first we met she is bound to be, methinks, and not
in vain, the darling of my heart, sleeping in her april cot, within
her singachamer, with her greengageflavoured candywhistle
duetted to the crazyquilt, Isobel, she is so pretty, truth to tell,
wildwood's eyes and primarose hair, quietly, all the woods so
wild, in mauves of moss and daphnedews, how all so still she lay,
neath of the whitethorn, child of tree, like some losthappy leaf,
like blowing flower stilled, as fain would she anon, for soon again
'twill be, win me, woo me, wed me, ah weary me! deeply, now
evencalm lay sleeping;

Robbie Robertson

ALL LA GLORY

I want to hear pitter patter
Climb up your ladder now
It's time for you to dream away
For what a big day you've been through
You've done things that you wanted to do

All La Glory
I'm second story
Feel so tall
Like a prison wall
          That tall

I'm lookin for a star bright
To shine down your light now
And keep the little one safe and warm
Cause to her it's just a fantasy
And to me it's all a mystery

All La Glory
I'm second story
Feel so tall
Like a prison wall

And before the leaves all turn brown
Before they fall to the ground
You will find the harmony
Wait and see
Listen to the serenade
Little girl promenade now
You've got the sunshine in your hand
And maybe come some sweet day
You'll walk that Milky Way

All La Glory
I'm second story
Feel so tall
Like a prison wall
          That tall

Kenneth Patchen

MIRRU

I tiptoed into her sleep
And she was a little girl
Listening to her father clearing the snow
From the sidewalk in front of their house
And it was sweetly mixed-up
With funnypapers on Sunday morning
And black, surly-friendly tomcats
Smelling of New England and
Finnish bread but Finns talk too long
And little girls get tired and father calls
I'll be asleep before you will
And after a moment calls again
Aren't you asleep yet? and when you say no
He adds triumphantly
I told you I'd win, *I'm* asleep
Leaving you to puzzle over it
And later when she has nearly "grown-up"
Sitting with her mother in the warm kitchen
Reading Mystery Stories and father asking
Are you two going to stay up all night?
And her mother assuring him that
Just as soon as this chapter is finished
We'll stop but somehow they never did
And holding squirmy little flower-eyed rabbits

And watching for Santa Claus at the front door
While the snow swirled so prettily on the lawn
Like a white queen in a beautiful dress.

John Berryman

NINE DREAM SONGS

To the edge of Europe, the eighteenth edge,
the ancient edge, Henry sailed full of thought
and rich with high-wrought designs,
for a tranquil mind & to fulfil a pledge
he gave himself to end a labour, sought
but now his mind not finds

comformable itself to that forever
or any more of the stretch of Henry's years.
Strange & new outlines
blur the old project. Soon they dissever
the pen & the heart, the old heart with its fears
& the daughter for which it pines.

Fresh toils the lightning over the Liffey, wild
and the avenues, like Paris's, are rain
and Henry is here for a while
of many months, along with the squalls of a child,
thirty years later. I will not come again
or not come with this style.

These nine Dream Songs (numbers 379, 271, 303, 131, 132, 293, 298, 330, and 385 respectively) are taken from *His Toy, His Dream, His Rest*. "Henry" is one of Berryman's many personae in this work.

Why then did he make, at such cost, *crazy* sounds?
to waken ancient longings, to remind (of childness),
to make laugh, and to hurt,
is and was all he ever intended. Short
came his commands.
Today, in April, the clouds have personalities. Yes,

there's a lamb one; that's lying down; he waits
his frightful chances; she hangs over; there's a dove;
two are conspiring;
one flies, wild. These banks and ranks of glowing cloud require
his passioning attention. Throng the Fates,
he couldn't care less, being in love

with his own teeming lady,—whose dorsal fin
is keeping her nauseous. Wait till that kid
comes out, I'll fix her.
I'll burp her till she bleeds, I'll take an ax
to her inability to focus, until in
one weird moment I fall in love with her too.

THREE IN HEAVEN I HOPE

'Three in heaven I hope' said old Jane to Henry
'and one in a mental hospital and three wed.'
Henry had only three.
Jack's lounge roared around them   they chatted over their
   kids,
Ten-thirty. Work's over, except Henry's: more.
The Irish clouds outside giving us an Irish downpour.

The baby in her high & hurried voice
babbles while Henry rocks & rocks; aged four.
I do love that baby.
Of babies I have loved I declare I rejoice
chiefly in Paul & Martha, called Twissy-Pits,
and jack-knifed how on the floor she sits

doing her colouring & her scissoring.
Brought Jerry with me home last night, Kate got cross,
Jerry likes my baby too.
Working & children & pals are the point of the thing,
for the grand sea awaits us, which will then us toss
& endlessly us undo.

Come touch me baby in his waking dream
disordered Henry murmured. I'll read you Hegel
and that will hurt your mind
I can't remember when you were unkind
but I will clear that block, I'll set you on fire
along with our babies

to save them up the high & ruined stairs,
my growing daughters. I am insane, I think,
they say & act so.
But then they let me out, and I must save them,
High fires will help, at this time, in my affairs.
I am insane, I know

and many of my close friends were half-sane
I see the rorschach for the dead on its way
Prop them up!
Trade us a lesson, pour me down a sink
I swear I'll love her always, like a drink
Let pass from me this cup

A SMALL DREAM

It was only a small dream of the Golden World,
now you trot off to bed. I'll turn the machine off,
you've danced & trickt us enough.
Unintelligible whines & imprecations, hurled
from the second floor, fail to impress your mother
and I am the only other

and I say go to bed! We'll meet tomorrow,
acres of threats dissolve into a smile,
you'll be the *Little* Baby
again, while I pursue my path of sorrow
& bodies, bodies, to be carried a mile
& dropt. Maybe

if frozen slush will represent the soul
which is to represented in the hereafter
I ask for a decree
dooming my bitter enemies to laughter
advanced against them. If the dream was small
it was my dream also, Henry's.

What gall had he in him, so to begin Book VII
or to design, out of its hotspur materials,
its ultimate structure
whereon will critics browse at large, at Heaven Eleven
finding it was not cliffhangers or old serials
but according to his nature.

O the baby has had one million & thirteen falls,
no wonder she howls
She'll trip on the steps at Vassar, ho, & bawl
in Latin. That baby has got to learn things
including remaining erect & on deck & all,
her study of herself must include no wings.

She's sturdy, beautiful, & she will do, unless
the universal homage turns her head
as it well might do mine,
hypmotized by the Little Baby, who has ears only for Diana
  & The Beast,
& mommy, & admirers & her Mir, instead
of brothers & sisters coming on like swine.

Henry in transition, transient Henry,
rubbed his eyes & hurt. He was on TV
with his baby daughter,
and Housman's rhyme O in this case was 'oughter
and Henry did his bloody level best
for all them young Englishmen & so did his daughter.

The baby on a million screens, hurrah,
my almost perfect child, in the midst of the cameramen
& Daddy's high-lit reading.
She never made a peep to that sensitive mike
my born performer. We'll see her through Smith & then
swiftly into the Senate.

Daddy by then will be the nearest ghost,
honey, but won't return. Daddy's heart sank
at leaving the lovely baby.
Your Mommy will be with you, when Henry's a blank,
you'll have to study him in school, at most,
troubled & gone Henry.

The Twiss is a tidy bundle, chirped joyous Henry,
all other dreams forgotten. Acres of joy
spring when she strode the bike
behind her mother, all so near the sea
where never she has been. A little boy
is what is Daddy's mike,

that which he seeks & fears ha ha. He's *supposed* to fear,
since everyone else does, but actually he can't make it.
He broadcasts freely.
Cantons of candy for the Little Twiss here.
She won a prize on board, one at the church,
at the supermarket

& in the hotel she was extravagantly admired,
I wonder it doesn't turn her silly head,
the little baby.
Universal clouds, an Irish sky,
said what would be her fate, tears & a child
and a father old & wild.

My daughter's heavier. Light leaves are flying.
Everywhere in enormous numbers turkeys will be dying
and other birds, all their wings.
They never greatly flew. Did they wish to?
I should know. Off away somewhere once I knew
such things.

Or good Ralph Hodgson back then did, or does.
The man is dead whom Eliot praised. My praise
follows and flows too late.
Fall is grievy, brisk. Tears behind the eyes
almost fall. Fall comes to us as a prize
to rouse us toward our fate.

My house is made of wood and it's made well,
unlike us. My house is older than Henry;
that's fairly old.
If there were a middle   ground between things and the soul
or if the sky resembled more the sea,
I wouldn't have to scold

                              my heavy daughter.

Robert Lowell

HOME AFTER THREE MONTHS AWAY

Gone now the baby's nurse,
a lioness who ruled the roost
and made the Mother cry.
She used to tie
gobbets of porkrind in bowknots of gauze—
three months they hung like soggy toast
on our eight foot magnolia tree,
and helped the English sparrows
weather a Boston winter.

Three months, three months!
Is Richard now himself again?
Dimpled with exaltation,
my daughter holds her levee in the tub.
Our noses rub,
each of us pats a stringy lock of hair—
they tell me nothing's gone.
Though I am forty-one,
not forty now, the time I put away
was child's-play. After thirteen weeks
my child still dabs her cheeks
to start me shaving. When
we dress her in her sky-blue corduroy,
she changes to a boy,
and floats my shaving brush
and washcloth in the flush. . . .
Dearest, I cannot loiter here
in lather like a polar bear.

Recuperating, I neither spin nor toil.
Three stories down below,
a choreman tends our coffin's length of soil,
and seven horizontal tulips blow.
Just twelve months ago,

these flowers were pedigreed
imported Dutchmen; now no one need
distinguish them from weed.
Bushed by the late spring snow,
they cannot meet
another year's snowballing enervation.

I keep no rank nor station.
Cured, I am frizzled, stale and small.

Stanley Kunitz

JOURNAL FOR MY DAUGHTER

1

Your turn. Grass of confusion.
You say you had a father once:
his name was absence.
He left, but did not let you go.
Part of him, more than a shadow,
beckoned down corridors,
secret, elusive, saturnine,
melting at your touch.
In the crack
of a divided house
grew the resentment-weed.
It has white inconspicuous flowers.
Family of anthologists!
Collectors of injuries!

2

I wake to a glittering world,
to the annunciation of the frost.
A popeyed chipmunk scurries past,
the pockets of his cheeks bulging.
As the field mice store seeds,
as the needle-nosed shrew
threading under the woodpile
deposits little heaps of land-snails
for milestones on its runways,
I propose
that we gather our affections,
Lambkin, I care.

3

I was happy you were born,
your banks of digits
equipped for decimals,
and all your clever parts
neatly in place.
Your nation gives me joy,
as it has always given.
If I could have my choice
on the way to exile
I think I'd rather sleep forever
than wake up cold
in a country without women.

4

You cried. You cried.
You wasted and you cried.
Night after night
I walked the floor with you,
croaking the same old
tranquillizing song,
the only tune
I ever learned to carry.
In the rosy tissue
of your brain,
where memory begins,
that theme is scored,
waiting till you need
to play it back.
There were three crows
sat on a tree
Sing Billy Magee Magaw.
You do not need to sing to me.
I like the sound of your voice
even when you phone from school
asking for money.

5

There was a big blond uncle-bear,
wounded, smoke-eyed, wild,
who shambled from the west
with his bags full of havoc.
He spoke the bears' grunt-language,
waving his paws
and rocking on his legs.
Both of us were drunk,
slapping each other on the back,
sweaty with genius.
He spouted his nonsense-rhymes,
roaring like a behemoth.
You crawled under the sofa.

6

Goodies are shaken
from the papa-tree:
Be what you are. Give
what is yours to give.
Have style. Dare.
Such a storm of fortune cookies!
Outside your room
stands the white-headed prowler
in his multiple disguises
who reminds you of your likeness.
Wherever you turn,
down whatever street,
in the fugues of appetite,
in the groin of nightmare,
he waits for you,
haggard with his thousand years.
His agents are everywhere,
his heart is at home
in your own generation;
the folded message in his hands
is stiff with dirt and wine-stains,

older than the Dead Sea Scrolls.
Daughter, read:
What do I want of my life?
More! More!

7

Demonstrations in the streets.
I am there not there,
ever uneasy in a crowd.
But you belong,
flaunting your home-made
insubordinate flag.
Why should I be surprised?
We come of a flinty maverick line.
In my father's time, I'm told,
our table was set in turn
for Maxim Gorky, Emma Goldman,
and the atheist Ingersoll.
If your slogan is mis-spelt
Don't tred on me!
still it strikes
parents and politicians down.
Noli me tangere! is what
I used to cry in Latin once.
Oh to be radical, young, desirable, cool!

8

Your first dog was a Pekinese,
fat and saucy Ko San,
half mandarin, half mini-lion,
who chased milkmen and mailmen
and bit the tires of every passing car
till a U.S. Royal hit him back.
You sobbed for half an hour,
then romped to the burial service
in the lower garden
by the ferny creek.

I helped you pick the stones
to mark his shallow grave.
It was the summer I went away.
One night I carried you outdoors,
in a blitz of fireflies,
to watch your first eclipse.
Your far-off voice,
drugged with milk and sleep,
said it was a leaf
sliding over the light.

9

The night when Coleridge,
heavy-hearted,
bore his crying child outside,
he noted
that those brimming eyes
caught the reflection
of the starry sky,
and each suspended tear
made a sparkling moon.

Anonymous

THE MAIDEN'S BEST ADORNING

Dear child, these words which briefly I declare,
Let them not hang like jewels in thine ear;
But in the secret closet of thine heart,
Lock them up safe, that they may ne'er depart.

Give first to God the flower of thy youth;
Take Scripture for thy guide, that word of truth;
Adorn thy soul with grace; prize wisdom more
Than all the pearls upon the Indian shore.
Think not to live still free from grief and sorrow:
That man who laughs today, may weep tomorrow.
Nor dream of joys unmixed, here below:
No roses here, but what on thorns do grow.

Let not thy winged days be spent in vain;
When gone, no gold will call them back again.
Strive to subdue thy sin, when first beginning;
Custom (when once confirmed) is strangely winning.
Be much in prayer: it is the begging-trade
By which true Christians are the richest made.

Be loving, patient, courteous, and kind:
So doing, thou shalt praise and honour find
Here upon earth; and when all-conquering death
Thy body shall dissolve, and stop thy breath,
Upon the golden wings of faith and love
Thy soul shall fly to paradise above.

This poem originally appeared on a broadside entitled *The Maidens Best Adorning: or, A Directory for the Female-Sex; being A Fathers Advice to his Daughter*, printed in London in 1687.

Robert Herrick

MY DAUGHTER'S DOWRY

Ere I go hence and be no more
Seen to the world, I'll quit the score
I owe unto a female child;
And that is this—a verse instyled
My Daughter's Dowry; having which,
I'll leave her then completely rich.

Instead of gold, pearls, rubies, bonds,
Long forfeited pawned diamonds,
Or antique pledges, house, or land,
I give thee this, that shall withstand
The blow of Ruin and of Chance.
These hurt not thine inheritance,
For 'tis fee simple; and no rent
Thou Fortune ow'st for tenement.
However after times will 'praise
This portion, my Prophetic Bays
Cannot deliver up to th' trust;
Yet I sleep pleased in my dust.
As for thy birth and better seeds—
Those which must grow to Virtuous Deeds—
Thou didst derive from this old stem
Love, Peace, and Mercy: cherish them.
Which, like a Vestal Virgin, ply
With holy fire lest it die.
Grow up by mild means to know
At what time to say aye and no.
Let manners teach thee where to be
More comely flowing, where less free.
These bring thy husband like to those
Old coins and medals we expose
To the sight but never part with. Next,
As in a more conspicuous text
(The forehead), let therein be sign'd

The maiden candor of thy mind;
And under it, two chaste-born spies
To bar out bold adulteries
(For through those optics pass the darts
Of lust which set on fire our hearts.)
On either side of these, quick ears
There must be plac'd to season fears,
Which sweeten love, yet ne'er come nigh
The brands of wilder jealousy.
    Then let each cheek of thine intice
His soul, as to a bed of spice
Where he may roll and loose his sense
As in a cloud of frankincense.
    A lip enkindled with that coal
With which love warms and chafes the soul
Bring to him next; and in it show
Love's cherries from such fires grow
And have their harvest—which must stand
The gathering of the lip, not hand.
    Then unto these, be it thy care
To clothe thy words in gentle air
That, smooth as oil, sweet, soft, and clean
As is the childish bloom of bean,
They may fall down and stroke, as the
Beams of the sun the peaceful sea.
    White hands as smooth as mercies bring
Him for his better cherishing,
That, when thou dost his neck ensnare
Or with thy wrist or fettering hair,
He may, a prisoner, there discry
Bondage more loved than liberty.
    A nature so well form'd, so wrought
To calm and temper, let be brought
With thee, that should he but incline
'To roughness, clasp him like a vine.
Or like as wool meets steel, give way
Unto the passion, not it stay:
(Wrath, if resisted, over-boils;
If not, it dies, or else recoils).

And lastly, see thou bring to him
Somewhat peculiar in each limb.
And I do charge thee to be known
By n' other face than by thine own.
Let it, in love's name, be kept sleek,
Yet to be found when he shall seek
It, and not, instead of saint,
Give up his worship to the paint.
For, trust me girl, she overdoes
Who by a double proxy woos.
But, lest I should forget his bed,
Be sure thou bring'st a maidenhead
That is a margarite; which, lost,
Thou bring'st into his bed a frost
Or a cold poison, which his blood
Benumbs like that forgetful flood.
Now, for some jewels to supply
The want of ear-ring bravery:
For public eyes, take only these,
Ne'er travelled for beyond the seas
(They're nobly home-bred, yet have price
Beyond the far fetcht merchandize):
Obedience, wise distrust, peace. Shy
Distance and sweet urbanity,
Safe modesty, love, patience, fear
Of offending, temperance, dear
Constancy, bashfulness, and all
The virtues less or cardinal
Take, with my blessing; and go forth
Injewelled with thy native worth.
And now, if there a man be found
That looks for such prepared ground,
Let him but with indifferent skill
So good a soil bestock and till,
    He may ere long, with such a wife,
    Nourish in's breast a Tree of Life.

Charles Plymell

FOR CYNARA

Once the poet goes behind the shades
once he draws the curtains
once the curtain of life is torn
once the certainty that eats
away the hours of the wall
and the wallpaper torn
to the pattern of the times.
Each pattern torn away or
stained to suit one's fancy
the impression of a day
the near tide of your face
the memory washes back
into my eyes.
The Child near the tide
the innocence of hours wind.
My memory of you has been long
while I am lost in continuous repair.

Robert Creeley

"FOR SOME WEEKS ..."
for Kirsten

For some weeks
now, caught in my
own complexities, I'd

been thinking
of you, first as
to have your

first child, then
(since not to) as
a woman now

entirely. My
own life, I
thought, this curious

space suit one
lives in, becomes
insistent also.

Think
of Andean flutes
filling the room

with mountains no less!
Dancing, you can
see the goats above you.

Or is it water,
as ever, one feels the
flooding of?

"Liquid notes"—
passion so articulately
carefree, as last.

I've been eating
too much. At times
I feel my stomach

will burst into the room.
My eye seems
to blur at close print.

Pieces
fall away dis-
closing another place.

These faces,
younger, a letter
from someone unknown,

collect much as
whatever would
falling off.

My mother comes
to visit soon. This
part of the country,

New England,
is most her home—
in ways not mine.

I remember
sitting in my sister's
dining-room in Berkeley

with you both
either side—a
warm and open

sunlit day. Possibly
we'll both wander
a long way.

When you first
left home, I had
fears—now

pride fills me,
a man with
a daughter a woman.

Happiness to you,
bless the world
you're given.

Robert Creeley

SITTING HERE

Roof's peak is eye,
sky's grey, tree's
a stack of lines,

wires across it. This
is window, this is
sitting at the table,

thinking of you,
far away,
whose face is

by the mirror on the bureau.
I love you, I said,
because I wanted to,

because I know you,
my daughter, my
daughter.

I don't want you
to walk away. I
get scared

in this loneliness.
Be *me* again
being born, be the little

wise one walks
quietly by, in the sun,
smiles silently,

grows taller and taller.
Because all these things
passing, changing,

all the things
coming and going
inside, outside—

I can't hold them,
I want to but
keep on losing them.

As if to catch your hand, then,
your fingers, to hang on,
as if to feel

it's all right here
and will be, that
world *is* wonder,

being simply beyond us,
patience its savor,
and to keep moving,

we love what we love,
what we have,
what we have to.

I don't know—
this fact of time spinning,
days, weeks, months, years,

stuffed in some attic.
Or—where can we run,
why do I want to?

As if that touch of you
had, unknowing,
turned me around again

truly to face you,
and your face is wet,
blurred, with tears—

or is it simply years later,
sitting here, and whatever
we were has gone.

Horace Gregory

STANZAS FOR MY DAUGHTER

Tell her I love
            she will remember me
always, for she
is of love's graces made;
                she will remember
these streets where the moon's shade
falls and my shadow mingles
with shadows sprung
from a midnight tree.

Tell her I love that I
am neither in earth nor sky,
stone nor cloud,
but only this
walled garden she knows well
and which her body is.

Her eyes alone shall make
me blossom for her sake;
contained within her, all
my days shall flower or die,
birthday or funeral
concealed where no man's eye
finds me unless she says:
He is my flesh and I
am what he was.

Live beyond hope,
            beyond October trees
spent with fire, these
ministers of false Spring
                making our bodies stir
with spurious flowering
under snow that covers

hope and hopeful lovers
and fades in timeless seas.

Live beyond hope, my care
that makes a prison for your eyes (and hair
golden as autumn grass
swept by the morning sun)
for you shall walk with praise
when all my ways are run.

Take all my love, but spend
such love to build your mind
against hope that leaves behind
my winter night and snow
falling at the year's end.

Tell her I know
                that living is too long
for our love to endure;
the tenuous and strong
web of time (outlasting
girls and men—love's rapid signature
of hand and lip and eye)
gleams as if wires were strung
across a sunset sky.

Tell her that girls and men
are shadows on the grass
where time's four seasons pass;
tell her that I have seen
                O many a nervous queen
of girls (Madonna, glorious)
white-towered goddess) fade
while walking in noon's shade,
separate limbs and foreheads bright,
now dim, anonymous. . . .

Tell her I love
           to make these words a song
with her careful lips,
              O bride,
Spring and bridegroom at your side,
save them for the deep and long
silences when northstar light
perishes down quicksilver steep
walls of flesh where love and death
make a counterfeit of sleep.

Take this wreath to celebrate
union of the fire and rain,
bone and tissue.
            Sleep, O bride,
for the walking limbs divide
into separate walls again.

Tell her that flesh is spirited
into earth:
           this wreath is grown
from black bronze roots to weave a crown
for the death mask and the head
fixed with its metallic smile
upward where generations climb
making garlands of their own
out of iron and of stone.

David Ignatow

FOR MY DAUGHTER IN REPLY TO A QUESTION

We're not going to die,
we'll find a way.
We'll breathe deeply
and eat carefully.
We'll think always on life.
There'll be no fading for you or for me.
We'll be the first
and we'll not laugh at ourselves ever
and your children will be my grandchildren.
Nothing will have changed
except by addition.
There'll never be another as you
and never another as I.
No one ever will confuse you
nor confuse me with another.
We will not be forgotten and passed over
and buried under the births and deaths to come.

David Ignatow

FOR MY DAUGHTER

When I die choose a star
and name it after me
that you may know
I have not abandoned
or forgotten you.
You were such a star to me,
following you through birth
and childhood, my hand
in your hand.
When I die
choose a star and name it
after me so that I may shine
down on you, until you join
me in darkness and silence
together.

I sleep so that in the silence
I can more clearly understand
myself. In darkness
I grope to the center
of my pulsation and find
to my dismay
a beating heart.

We are here to make each other die
with perfect willingness.
It is like flagellants
who strike each other methodically
with straps.
Lying in blood
upon the floor they have reached
the climax they were seeking:
to be destroyed and delighted
at the same time
from the same source.

Yvor Winters

AT THE SAN FRANCISCO AIRPORT
To my daughter, 1954

This is the terminal: the light
Gives perfect vision, false and hard;
The metal glitters, deep and bright.
Great planes are waiting in the yard—
They are already in the night.

And you are here beside me, small,
Contained and fragile, and intent
On things that I but half recall—
Yet going whither you are bent.
I am the past, and that is all.

But you and I in part are one:
The frightened brain, the nervous will,
The knowledge of what must be done,
The passion to acquire the skill
To face that which you dare not shun.

The rain of matter upon sense
Destroys me momently. The score:
There comes what will come. The expense
Is what one thought, and something more—
One's being and intelligence.

This is the terminal, the break.
Beyond this point, on lines of air,
You take the way that you must take;
And I remain in light and stare—
In light, and nothing else, awake.

Vinícius de Moraes

SONG
Translated by Richard Wilbur

Never take her away,
The daughter whom you gave me,
The gentle, moist, untroubled
Small daughter whom you gave me;
O let her heavenly babbling
Beset me and enslave me.
Don't take her; let her stay,
Beset my heart, and win me,
That I may put away
The firstborn child within me,
That cold, petrific, dry
Daughter whom death once gave,
Whose life is a long cry
For milk she may not have,
And who, in the night-time, calls me
In the saddest voice that can be
Father, Father, and tells me
Of the love she feels for me.
Don't let her go away,
Her whom you gave—my daughter—
Lest I should come to favor
That wilder one, that other
Who does not leave me ever.

Vinícius de Moraes is the contemporary Brazilian poet and song writer.
He wrote the screenplay for *Black Orpheus*.

Paul Goodman

MY DAUGHTER VERY ILL

My little darling looked so pale today
   fading away
pining and thin like the transparent moon
   in the afternoon,
I cannot sleep, obsessed by Susie's colorless
   cheerless face
and bony body in my arms too light,
   she who was bright
comparable to the meadowflowers
   alas! that the mowers
passed and did not spare, their petals droop
   my shoulders stoop
for fear and neither can I breathe for fear.

   No, hear my prayer,
Nature! who alone healest and not wishes
   nor art nor pity,
and do thou Creator Spirit visit her
   with the quick future
that alone stirs to courage and to walk
   and to work.

Ben Jonson

ON MY FIRST DAUGHTER

Here lyes to each her parents ruth,
Mary, the daughter of their youth:
Yet, all heavens gifts, being heavens due,
It makes the father, lesse, to rue.
At sixe moneths end, shee parted hence
With safetie of her innocence;
Whose soule heavens Queene, (whose name shee beares)
In comfort of her mothers teares,
Hath plac'd amongst her virgin-traine:
Where, while that sever'd doth remaine,
This grave partakes the fleshly birth.
Which cover lightly, gentle earth.

Kenneth Patchen

PETER'S LITTLE DAUGHTER DIES

That she must change so soon her curving city;
Leave this travel scarcely started; never see
Stars again reposeful in that dear room
Where death strays not and little birds
Are never split by shot—is it like this,
Dying? Just the moment going over
The edge of body, nothing left there
That grass cannot solve?

I'd wish to settle nothing here with chisel;
No cold angel with well-fed eyes shall rest above her . . .
She once said "The Snow Queen must be very beautiful."

She was so tiny . . . She won't know what the dead are
    supposed to do.

Hawaiian Song

DIRGE
Translated by Armand Schwerner

I make this dirge for you Miss Mary Binning I miss you
o my daughter the wind of Na'alehu used to scatter dust in
    our house
o my daughter at the Lau-hu cliff
I'm crying for missing you and let it be; I love you I see us
o my daughter at the cold Ka-puna spring our water, in the
    rain
that the Ha'ao hill undergoes
up the trail almost nobody knew, us alone o my daughter
I'm missing you my life turns
a shade greyer forever
it's over now, you on your road endlessly who used to shine so
    my darling,
now in the one direction, away, me still in these places,
on a walk, up a hill, next to the spring dampening me, bent
from this stone yearning
                o precious
as pearls, in Waikapuna the sun warmed you I didn't know
    you
from the flowers

"Dirge" is Armand Schwerner's "working" and adaptation of a translation made by Handy and Pakui in the *Journal of the Polynesian Society.*
Shortly before *The Roses Race Around Her Name* went to press,
Schwerner informed me that this particular poem was in fact a mother's
lament for her daughter. The one "exception" to the principle of selection adopted for this anthology, this poem has been included in accor-
dance with Emerson's idea that "a foolish consistency is the hobgoblin of
little minds."

John Lennon and Paul McCartney

SHE'S LEAVING HOME

Wednesday morning at five o'clock as the day begins
Silently closing her bedroom door
Leaving the note that she hoped would say more
She goes downstairs to the kitchen clutching her handkerchief
Quietly turning the backdoor key
Stepping outside she is free.

She
    (we gave her most of our lives)
Is leaving
      (sacrificed most of our lives)
Home
    (we gave her everything money could buy)
She's leaving home after living alone
For so many years.
          Bye, bye.

Father snores as his wife gets into her dressing gown
Picks up the letter that's lying there
Standing alone at the top of the stairs
She breaks down and cries to her husband:
Daddy our baby's gone
Why would she treat us so thoughtlessly
How could she do this to me.

She
    (we never thought of ourselves)
Is leaving
      (never a thought for ourselves)
Home
    (we struggled hard all our lives to get by)
She's leaving home after living alone
For so many years.
          Bye, bye.

Friday morning at nine o'clock she is far away
Waiting to keep the appointment she made
Meeting a man from the motor trade.
She
    (what did we do that was wrong)
Is having
        (we didn't know it was wrong)
Fun
    (fun is the one thing that money can't buy)
Something inside that was always denied
For so many years. Bye, bye.
She's leaving home.
        Bye, bye.

Stephen Spender

MISSING MY DAUGHTER

This wall-paper has lines that rise
Upright like bars, and overhead,
The ceiling's patterned with red roses.
On the wall opposite the bed
The staring looking-glass encloses
Six roses in its white of eyes.

Here at my desk, with note-book open
Missing my daughter, makes those bars
Draw their lines upward through my mind.
This blank page stares at me like glass
Where stared-at roses wish to pass
Through petalling of my pen.

An hour ago, there came an image
Of a beast that pressed its muzzle
Between bars. Next, through tick and tock
Of the reiterating clock
A second glared with the wide dazzle
Of deserts. The door, in a green mirage,

Opened. In my daughter came.
Her eyes were wide as those she has,
The round gaze of her childhood was
White as the distance in the glass
Or on a white page, a white poem.
The roses raced around her name.

D. H. Lawrence

BABY-MOVEMENTS

I

Running Barefoot

When the white feet of the baby beat across the grass
White flowers in the wind bob up and down.
And ripples poise and run, lapping across the water.
The sight of their white play among the grass,
Is like a little linnet song, winsome,
Is like when two white butterflies settle in the arms of one
    flower
For a moment, then away with a flutter of wings.
    I wait for the baby to wander hither to me,
Like a wind-shadow wandering over the water,
So she may stand on my knee
With her two bare feet on my hands
Cool as syringa buds
Cool and firm and silken as pink young peony flowers.

"Running Barefoot" and "Trailing Clouds" are early versions of "Baby
Running Barefoot" and "A Baby Asleep After Pain" respectively. These
poems were apparently inspired by Hilda Mary Jones, the baby
daughter of Mr. and Mrs. T.W. Jones, at whose house Lawrence resided
when he was teaching at Croydon in 1908.

II

Trailing Clouds

As a drenched, drowned bee
Hangs numb and heavy from the bending flower,
   So clings to me,
My baby, her brown hair brushed with wet tears
   And laid laughterless on her cheek,
Her soft white legs hanging heavily over my arm
   Swinging to my lullaby.
My sleeping baby hangs upon my life
   As a silent bee at the end of a shower
   Draws down the burdened flower.
She who has always seemed so light
   Sways on my arm like sorrowful, storm-heavy boughs,
Even her floating hair sinks like storm-bruised young leaves
Reaching downwards:
   As the wings of a drenched, drowned bee
   Are a heaviness, and a weariness.

James Joyce

A FLOWER GIVEN TO MY DAUGHTER

Frail the white rose and frail are
Her hands that gave
Whose soul is sere and paler
Than time's wan wave.

Rosefrail and fair—yet frailest
A wonder wild
In gentle eyes thou veilest,
My blueveined child.

Gary Snyder

KYOTO BORN IN SPRING SONG

Beautiful little children
    found in melons,
    in bamboo,
  in a "strangely glowing warbler egg"
    a perfect baby girl—

baby, baby,
    tiny precious
      mice and worms:

    Great majesty of Dharma turning
    Great dance of Vajra power

lizard baby by the fern
centipede baby scrambling toward the wall
cat baby left to mew for milk alone
mouse baby too afraid to run

      O sing born in spring
    the weavers swallows babies in Nishijin
      nests below the eaves

      glinting mothers wings
      swoop to the sound of looms

    and three fat babies
  with three human mothers
every morning doing laundry
          "good
morning how's your baby?"
Tomoharu, Itsuko, and Kenji—

    Mouse, begin again.

Bushmen are laughing
  at the coyote-tricking
    that made us think machines
  wild babies
in the ferns and plums and weeds.

Nathaniel Tarn

BRING A CHILD FLOWERS

Bring a child flowers: pluck them from the air,
cut them in gardens, buy them at corner stalls,
smart shops — all one. Her smile is of one price.

If you can explain to me how it comes about
that one can adore so and wish to cripple so
in one same moment one's own life's fingers,
one's mornings' reapers, the weavers of one's nights —
I think some other poet said: I love, and hate
and I am miserable without understanding of this human state—
tell me with this one smile how it can be.

When I can still my nerve to her pace,
she is such gold, such reward,
not shrill at all.

The border of heaven and hell this very moment
(though I'm full of good will to bursting) reels on a nerve
which falls like a rod straight through my guts.
We do not go from health into disease
and back again to health. We crawl like animals,
nursing the worms will eat them later on,
from pain to pain. And pain's nerve runs here:

a frontier on which love and rage confuse their documents,
a no man's land in which the pass of love
meanders like my child from smiles to tears.

Do tell my children please, in black on white,
that once, when I was young and close to them,
I loved them as a god must love his fantasies
and laid my hands upon them while they slept,
willing my love to fashion in my hands
such rainbow sprays of covenanted time
as reached one season when, flower-like, they wilted
into the men and women who do not know me.

Lawrence Durrell

TO PING-KU, ASLEEP

You sleeping child asleep, away
Between the confusing world of forms,
The lamplight and the day; you lie
And the pause flows through you like glass,
Asleep in the body of the nautilus.

Between comparison and sleep,
Lips that move in quotation;
The turning of a small blind mind
Like a plant everywhere ascending.
Now our love has become a beanstalk.

Invent a language where the terms
Are smiles; someone in the house now
Only understands warmth and cherish,
Still twig-bound, learning to fly.

This hand exploring the world makes
The diver's deep-sea fingers on the sills
Of underwater windows; all the wrecks
Of our world where the sad blood leads back
Through memory and sense like divers working.

Sleep, my dear, we won't disturb
You, lying in the zones of sleep.
The four walls symbolise love put about
To hold in silence which so soon brims
Over into sadness: it's still dark.

Sleep and rise a lady with a flower
Between your teeth and a cypress
Between your thighs: surely you won't ever
Be puzzled by a poem or disturbed by a poem
Made like fire by the rubbing of two sticks?

William Wordsworth

THE LONGEST DAY

Let us quit the leafy arbour,
And the torrent murmuring by;
For the sun is in his harbour,
Weary of the open sky.

Evening now unbinds the fetters
Fashioned by the glowing light;
All that breathe are thankful debtors
To the harbinger of night.

Yet by some grave thoughts attended
Eve renews her calm career;
For the day that now is ended
Is the longest of the year.

Dora! sport, as now thou sportest,
On this platform, light and free;
Take thy bliss, while longest, shortest,
Are indifferent to thee!

Who would check the happy feeling
That inspires the linnet's song?
Who would stop the swallow, wheeling
On her pinions swift and strong?

Yet, at this impressive season,
Words which tenderness can speak
From the truths of homely reason
Might exalt the loveliest cheek;

This poem, written in 1817, is addressed to Wordsworth's daughter
Dora.

And, while shades to shades succeeding
Steal the landscape from the sight,
I would urge this moral pleading,
Last forerunner of 'Good night!'

Summer ebbs;—each day that follows
Is a reflux from on high,
Tending to the darksome hollows
Where the frosts of winter lie.

He who governs the creation,
In his providence, assigned
Such a gradual declination
To the life of human kind.

Yet we mark it not;—fruits redden,
Fresh flowers blow as flowers have blown,
And the heart is loath to deaden
Hopes that she so long hath known.

Be thou wiser, youthful Maiden!
And when thy decline shall come,
Let not flowers, or boughs fruit-laden,
Hide the knowledge of thy doom.

Now, even now, ere wrapped in slumber,
Fix thine eyes upon the sea
That absorbs time, space, and number;
Look thou to Eternity!

Follow thou the flowing river
On whose breast are thither borne
All deceived, and each deceiver,
Through the gates of night and morn;

Through the year's successive portals;
Through the bounds which many a star
Marks, not mindless of frail mortals,
When his light returns from far.

Thus when thou with Time hast travelled
Toward the mighty gulf of things,
And the mazy stream unravelled
With thy best imaginings;

Think, if thou on beauty leanest,
Think how pitiful that stay,
Did not virtue give the meanest
Charms superior to decay.

Duty, like a strict preceptor,
Sometimes frowns, or seems to frown;
Choose her thistle for thy sceptre,
While youth's roses are thy crown.

Grasp it,—if thou shrink and tremble,
Fairest damsel of the green,
Thou wilt lack the only symbol
That proclaims a genuine queen;

And ensures those palms of honour
Which selected spirits wear,
Bending low before the Donor,
Lord of heaven's unchanging year!

William Wordsworth

IT IS A BEAUTEOUS EVENING, CALM AND FREE

It is a beauteous evening, calm and free,
The holy time is quiet as a Nun
Breathless with adoration; the broad sun
Is sinking down in its tranquillity;
The gentleness of heaven broods o'er the Sea:
Listen! the mighty Being is awake,
And doth with his eternal motion make
A sound like thunder—everlastingly.
Dear Child! dear Girl! that walkest with me here,
If thou appear untouched by solemn thought,
Thy nature is not therefore less divine:
Thou liest in Abraham's bosom all the year;
And worshipp'st at the Temple's inner shrine,
God being with thee when we know it not.

This poem is addressed to Caroline, daughter of the poet and Annette Vallon.

William Wordsworth

CHARACTERISTICS OF A CHILD THREE YEARS OLD

Loving she is, and tractable, though wild;
And Innocence hath privilege in her
To dignify arch looks and laughing eyes;
And feats of cunning; and the pretty round
Of trespasses, affected to provoke
Mock-chastisement and partnership in play.
And, as a faggot sparkles on the earth,
Not less if unattended and alone
Than when both young and old sit gathered round
And take delight in its activity;
Even so this happy Creature of herself
Is all-sufficient; solitude to her
Is blithe society, who fills the air
With gladness and involuntary songs.
Light are her sallies as the tripping fawn's
Forth-startled from the fern where she lay couched;
Unthought-of, unexpected, as the stir
Of the soft breeze ruffling the meadow-flowers,
Or from before it chasing wantonly
The many-coloured images imprest
Upon the bosom of a placid lake.

Addressed to Wordsworth's daughter Catherine, born in 1808.

William Wordsworth

SURPRISED BY JOY—IMPATIENT AS THE WIND

Surprised by joy—impatient as the Wind
I turned to share the transport—Oh! with whom
But Thee, deep buried in the silent tomb,
That spot which no vicissitude can find?
Love, faithful love, recalled thee to my mind—
But how could I forget thee? Through what power,
Even for the least division of an hour,
Have I been so beguiled as to be blind
To my most grievous loss!—That thought's return
Was the worst pang that sorrow ever bore,
Save one, one only, when I stood forlorn,
Knowing my heart's best treasure was no more;
That neither present time, nor years unborn
Could to my sight that heavenly face restore.

Addressed to Catherine, who died in 1812 at the age of four.

Bob Dylan

TEARS OF RAGE

We carried you in our arms
On Independence Day,
And now you'd throw us all aside
And put us on our way.
Oh what dear daughter beneath the sun
Would treat a father so,
To wait upon him hand and foot
And always tell him, No?
Tears of rage, tears of grief,
Why must I always be the thief?
Come to me now, you know
We're so alone
And life is brief.

We pointed out the way to go
And scratched your name in sand,
Though you just thought it was nothing more
Than a place for you to stand.
Now I want you to know that while we watched,
You discover there was no one true.
Most everybody really thought
It was a childish thing to do.
Tears of rage, tears of grief,
Must I always be the thief?
Come to me now, you know
We're so low
And life is brief.

"Tears of Rage" was written in 1967, the year Bob Dylan recorded and released a number of haunting songs on the now-famous underground "basement" tape—songs like "This Wheel's On Fire" and "Too Much of Nothing" whose intensity and imagery seem, in part, to be derived from a deep understanding of Shakespeare's *King Lear*: "Oh what dear daughter beneath the sun / Would treat a father so / To wait upon him hand and foot / And always tell him, No."

It was all very painless
When you went out to receive
All that false instruction
Which we never could believe.
And now the heart is filled with gold
As if it was a purse.
But, oh, what kind of love is this
Which goes from bad to worse?
Tears of rage, tears of grief,
Must I always be the thief?
Come to me now, you know
We're so low
And life is brief.

W. D. Snodgrass

HEART'S NEEDLE
For Cynthia

" 'Your father is dead.' 'That grieves me,' said
he. 'Your mother is dead,' said the lad. 'Now all
pity for me is at an end,' said he. 'Your brother
is dead,' said Loingsechan. 'I am sorely
wounded by that,' said Suibne. 'Your daughter
is dead,' said Loingsechan. 'And an only
daughter is the needle of the heart,' said
Suibne. 'Dead is your son who used to call you
"Father," ' said Loingsechan. 'Indeed,' said he,
'that is the drop that brings a man to the
ground.' "

FROM AN OLD IRISH STORY,
THE FRENZY OF SUIBNE,
AS TRANSLATED BY MYLES DILLON

1

Child of my winter, born
When the new fallen soldiers froze
In Asia's steep ravines and fouled the snows,
When I was torn

By love I could not still,
By fear that silenced my cramped mind
To that cold war where, lost, I could not find
My peace in my will,

All those days we could keep
Your mind a landscape of new snow
Where the chilled tenant-farmer finds, below,
His fields asleep.

In their smooth covering, white
As quilts to warm the resting bed
Of birth or pain, spotless as paper spread
For me to write,

And thinks: Here lies my hand
Unmarked by agony, the lean foot
Of the weasel tracking, the thick trapper's boot;
And I have planned

My chances to restrain
The torments of demented summer or
Increase the deepening harvest here before
It snows again.

2

Late April and you are three; today
   We dug your garden in the yard.
To curb the damage of your play,
Strange dogs at night and the moles tunneling,
   Four slender sticks of lath stand guard
      Uplifting their thin string.

So you were the first to tramp it down.
   And after the earth was sifted close
You brought your watering can to drown
All earth *and* us. But these mixed seeds are pressed
   With light loam in their steadfast rows.
      Child, we've done our best.

Someone will have to weed and spread
   The young sprouts. Sprinkle them in the hour
When the shadow falls across their bed.
You should try to look at them every day
   Because when they come to full flower
      I will be away.

3

The child between them on the street
Comes to a puddle, lifts his feet
   And hangs on their hands. They start
At the live weight and lurch together,
Recoil to swing him through the weather,
   Stiffen and pull apart.

We read of cold war soldiers that
Never gained ground, gave none, but sat
   Tight in their chill trenches.
Pain seeps up from some cavity
Through the ranked teeth in sympathy;
   The whole jaw grinds and clenches

Till something somewhere has to give.
It's better the poor soldiers live
   In someone else's hands
Than drop where helpless powers fall
On crops and barns, on towns where all
   Will burn. And no man stands.

For good, they sever and divide
Their won and lost land. On each side
   Prisoners are returned
Excepting a few unknown names.
The peasant plods back and reclaims
   His fields that strangers burned

And nobody seems very pleased.
It's best. Still, what must not be seized
   Clenches the empty fist.
I tugged your hand, once, when I hated
Things less: a mere game dislocated
   The radius of your wrist.

Love's wishbone, child, although I've gone
As men must and let you be drawn

Off to appease another,
It may help that a Chinese play
Or Solomon himself might say
   I am your real mother.

4

No one can tell you why
  the season will not wait;
    the night I told you I
must leave, you wept a fearful rate
      to stay up late.

Now that it's turning Fall,
  we go to take our walk
    among municipal
flowers, to steal one off its stalk,
      to try and talk.

We huff like windy giants
  scattering with our breath
    gray-headed dandelions;
Spring is the cold wind's aftermath.
      The poet saith.

But the asters, too, are gray,
  ghost-gray. Last night's cold
    is sending on their way
petunias and dwarf marigold,
      hunched sick and old.

Like nerves caught in a graph,
  the morning-glory vines
    frost has erased by half
still crawl across their rigid twines.
      Like broken lines

of verses I can't make.
  In its unraveling loom
    we find a flower to take,

with some late buds that might still bloom,
    back to your room.

    Night comes and the stiff dew.
  I'm told a friend's child cried
    because a cricket, who
had minstreled every night outside
    her window, died.

5

Winter again and it is snowing;
Although you are still three,
You are already growing
Strange to me.

You chatter about new playmates, sing
Strange songs; you do not know
Hey ding-a-ding-a-ding
Or where I go

Or when I sang for bedtime, *Fox*
Went out on a chilly night.
Before I went for walks
And did not write:

You never mind the squalls and storms
That are renewed long since:
Outside, the thick snow swarms
Into my prints

And swirls out by warehouses, sealed,
Dark cowbarns, huddled, still,
Beyond to the blank field,
The fox's hill

Where he backtracks and sees the paw,
Gnawed off, he cannot feel;
Conceded to the jaw
Of toothed, blue steel.

6

Easter has come around
again; the river is rising
    over the thawed ground
and the banksides. When you come you bring
    an egg dyed lavender.
We shout along our bank to hear
our voices returning from the hills to meet us.
    We need the landscape to repeat us.

You lived on this bank first.
While nine months filled your term, we knew
    how your lungs, immersed
in the womb, miraculously grew
    their useless folds till
the fierce, cold air rushed in to fill
them out like bushes thick with leaves. You took your hour,
    caught breath, and cried with your full lung power.

Over the stagnant bight
we see the hungry bank swallow
    flaunting his free flight
still; we sink in mud to follow
    the killdeer from the grass
that hides her nest. That March there was
rain; the rivers rose; you could hear killdeers flying
    all night over the mudflats crying.

You bring back how the red-
winged blackbird shrieked, slapping frail wings,
    diving at my head—
I saw where her tough nest, cradled, swings
    in tall reeds that must sway
with the winds blowing every way.
If you recall much, you recall this place. You still
    live nearby—on the opposite hill.

After the sharp windstorm
of July Fourth, all that summer
   through the gentle, warm
afternoons, we heard great chain saws chirr
   like iron locusts. Crews
of roughneck boys swarmed to cut loose
branches wrenched in the shattering wind, to hack free
   all the torn limbs that could sap the tree.

   In the debris lay
starlings, dead. Near the park's birdrun
   we surprised one day
a proud, tan-spatted, buff-brown pigeon.
   In my hands she flapped so
fearfully that I let her go.
Her keeper came. And we helped snarl her in a net.
   You bring things I'd as soon forget.

   You raise into my head
a Fall night that I came once more
   to sit on your bed;
sweat beads stood out on your arms and forehead and you wheezed for breath,
for help, like some child caught beneath
its comfortable woolly blankets, drowning there.
   Your lungs caught and would not take the air.

   Of all things, only we
have power to choose that we should die;
   nothing else is free
in this world to refuse it. Yet I,
   who say this, could not raise
myself from bed how many days
to the thieving world. Child, I have another wife,
   another child. We try to choose our life.

7

Here in the scuffled dust
  is our ground of play.
I lift you on your swing and must
  shove you away,
see you return again,
  drive you off again, then

stand quiet till you come.
  You, though you climb
higher, farther from me, longer
  will fall back to me stronger.
Bad penny, pendulum,
  you keep my constant time

to bob in blue July
  where fat goldfinches fly
over the glittering, fecund
  reach of our growing lands.
Once more now, this second,
  I hold you in my hands.

8

I thumped on you the best I could
    which was no use;
you would not tolerate your food
until the sweet, fresh milk was soured
    with lemon juice.

That puffed you up like a fine yeast.
    The first June in your yard
like some squat Nero at a feast
you sat and chewed on white, sweet clover.
    That is over.

When you were old enough to walk
    we went to feed
the rabbits in the park milkweed;
saw the paired monkeys, under lock,
    consume each other's salt.

Going home we watched the slow
stars follow us down Heaven's vault.
You said, let's catch one that comes low,
    pull off its skin
    and cook it for our dinner.

  As absentee bread-winner,
I seldom got you such cuisine;
we ate in local restaurants
or bought what lunches we could pack
    in a brown sack

with stale, dry bread to toss for ducks
    on the green-scummed lagoons,
crackers for porcupine and fox,
life-savers for the footpad coons
    to scour and rinse,

snatch after in their muddy pail
    and stare into their paws.
When I moved next door to the jail
    I learned to fry
omelettes and griddlecakes so I

could set you supper at my table.
As I built back from helplessness,
    when I grew able,
the only possible answer was
    you had to come here less.

This Hallowe'en you come one week.
        You masquerade
    as a vermilion, sleek,
fat, crosseyed fox in the parade
or, where grim jackolanterns leer,

go with your bag from door to door
foraging for treats. How queer:
    when you take off your mask
my neighbors must forget and ask
        whose child you are.

Of course you lose your appetite
    whine and won't touch your plate
        as local law
I set your place on an orange crate
in your own room for days. At night

you lie asleep there on the bed
        and grate your jaw.
Assuredly your father's crimes
        are visited
on you. You visit me sometimes.

The time's up. Now our pumpkin sees
    me bringing your suitcase.
        He holds his grin;
the forehead shrivels, sinking in.
You break this year's first crust of snow

off the runningboard to eat.
    We manage, though for days
I crave sweets when you leave and know
they rot my teeth. Indeed our sweet
        foods leave us cavities.

9

I get numb and go in
though the dry ground will not hold
    the few dry swirls of snow
and it must not be very cold.
A friend asks how you've been
    and I don't know

    or see much right to ask.
Or what use it could be to know.
    In three months since you came
the leaves have fallen and the snow;
your pictures pinned above my desk
    seem much the same.

Somehow I come to find
myself upstairs in the third floor
    museum's halls,
walking to kill my time once more
among the enduring and resigned
    stuffed animals,

    where, through a century's
caprice, displacement and
    known treachery between
its wars, they hear some old command
and in their peaceable kingdoms freeze
    to this still scene,

    Nature Morte. Here
by the door, its guardian
    the patchwork dodo stands
where you and your stepsister ran
laughing and pointing. Here, last year,
    you pulled my hands

and had your first, worst quarrel,
so toys were put up on your shelves.
   Here in the first glass cage
the little bobcats arch themselves,
still practicing their snarl
     of constant rage.

   The bison, here, immense,
shoves at his calf, brow to brow,
   and looks it in the eye
to see what is it thinking now.
I forced you to obedience;
     I don't know why.

   Still the lean lioness
beyond them, on her jutting ledge
   of shale and desert shrub,
stands watching always at the edge,
stands hard and tanned and envious
     above her cub;

   with horns locked in tall heather,
two great Olympian Elks stand bound,
   fixed in their lasting hate
till hunger brings them both to ground.
Whom equal weakness binds together
     none shall separate.

   Yet separate in the ocean
of broken ice, the white bear reels
   beyond the leathery groups
of scattered, drab Arctic seals
arrested here in violent motion
     like Napoleon's troops.

Our states have stood so long
At war, shaken with hate and dread,
   they are paralyzed at bay;
once we were out of reach, we said,
we would grow reasonable and strong.
   Some other day.

Like the cold men of Rome,
we have won costly fields to sow
   in salt, our only seed.
Nothing but injury will grow.
I write you only the bitter poems
   that you can't read.

Onan who would not breed
a child to take his brother's bread
   and be his brother's birth,
rose up and left his lawful bed,
went out and spilled his seed
   in the cold earth.   .

I stand by the unborn,
by putty-colored children curled
   in jars of alcohol,
that waken to no other world,
unchanging where no eye shall mourn.
   I see the caul

that wrapped a kitten, dead.
I see the branching, doubled throat
   of a two-headed foal;
I see the hydrocephalic goat;
here is the curled and swollen head,
   there, the burst skull:

skin of a limbless calf;
a horse's foetus, mummified;
    mounted and joined forever,
the Siamese twin dogs that ride
belly to belly, half and half,
        that none shall sever.

I walk among the growths,
by gangrenous tissue, goitre, cysts,
    by fistulas and cancers,
where the malignancy man loathes
is held suspended and persists.
    And I don't know the answers.

The window's turning white.
The world moves like a diseased heart
    packed with ice and snow.
Three months now we have been apart
less than a mile. I cannot fight
        or let you go.

10

The vicious winter finally yields
    the green winter wheat;
the farmer, tired in the tired fields
    he dare not leave will eat.

Once more the runs come fresh; prevailing
    piglets, stout as jugs,
harry their old sow to the railing
    to ease her swollen dugs.

and game colts trail the herded mares
    that circle the pasture courses;
our seasons bring us back once more
    like merry-go-round horses.

With crocus mouths, perennial hungers,
    into the park Spring comes;
we roast hot dogs on old coat hangers
    and feed the swan bread crumbs,

pay our respects to the peacocks, rabbits,
    and leathery Canada goose
who took, last Fall, our tame white habits
    and now will not turn loose.

In full regalia, the pheasant cocks
    march past their dubious hens;
the porcupine and the lean, red fox
    trot around bachelor pens

and the miniature painted train
    wails on its oval track:
you said, I'm going to Pennsylvania!
    and waved. And you've come back.

If I loved you, they said, I'd leave
    and find my own affairs.
Well, once again this April, we've
    come around to the bears;

punished and cared for, behind bars,
    the coons on bread and water
stretch thin black fingers after ours.
    And you are still my daughter.

William Butler Yeats

FATHER AND CHILD

She hears me strike the board and say
That she is under ban
Of all good men and women,
Being mentioned with a man
That has the worst of all bad names;
And thereupon replies
That his hair is beautiful,
Cold as the March wind his eyes.

Stephen Spender

TO MY DAUGHTER

Bright clasp of her whole hand around my finger,
My daughter, as we walk together now.
All my life I'll feel a ring invisibly
Circle this bone with shining: when she is grown
Far from today as her eyes are far already.

Stéphane Mallarmé

A FAN FOR HIS DAUGHTER
Translated by David Paul

Child, dreamer, that I may wind
A wayless path of pure delight,
Learn by the most delicate sleight
To keep my wing-tip in your hand.

A coolness, a breath of dusk
Comes to you with every beat
Whose imprisoned fluttering makes
The sky's distance palpitate.

See how dizzily space can swoon
Shivering like a giant kiss
That, wild at being born for no-one,
May neither close nor be at peace.

Feel the wild paradise retreat
Within the secret smile that escapes
Leapt from the parting of your lips
Into the fan's unanimous pleat!

This sceptre of the shores of rose,
Stilled above the golds of sunset,
Is the white, folded flight you poise
Against the fires of your bracelet.

The original title of this poem is *Autre Eventail* de *Mademoiselle Mallarmé.*

William Savage Landor

TO MY DAUGHTER

By that dejected city, Arno runs,
Where Ugolino claspt his famisht sons.
There wert thou born, my Julia! there thine eyes
Return'd as bright a blue to vernal skies.
And thence, my little wanderer! when the Spring
Advanced, thee, too, the hours on silent wing
Brought, while anemonies were quivering round,
And pointed tulips pierced the purple ground,
Where stood fair Florence: there thy voice first blest
My ear, and sank like balm into my breast:
For many griefs had wounded it, and more
Thy little hands could lighten were in store.
But why revert to griefs? Thy sculptured brow
Dispels from mine its darkest cloud even now.
What then the bliss to see again thy face,
And all that Rumour has announced of grace!
I urge, with fevered breast, the four-month day.
O! could I sleep to wake again in May.

Galway Kinnell

LITTLE SLEEP'S-HEAD
SPROUTING HAIR IN THE MOONLIGHT

1

You scream, waking from a nightmare.

When I sleepwalk
into your room, and pick you up,
and hold you up in the moonlight, you cling to me
hard,
as if clinging could save us. I think
you think
I will never die, I think I exude
to you the permanence of smoke or stars,
even as
my broken arms heal themselves around you.

2

I have heard you tell
the sun, *don't go down*, I have stood by
as you told the flower, *don't grow old,
don't die*. Little Maud,

I would blow the flame out of your silver cup,
I would suck the rot from your fingernail,
I would brush your sprouting hair of the dying light,
I would scrape the rust off your ivory bones,
I would help death escape through the little ribs of your body,
I would alchemize the ashes of your cradle back into wood,
I would let nothing of you go, ever,
until washerwomen
feel the clothes fall asleep in their hands,
and hens scratch their spell across hatchet blades,
and rats walk away from the cultures of the plague,

and iron twists weapons toward the true north,
and grease refuses to slide in the machinery of progress,
and men feel as free on earth as fleas on the bodies of men,
and lovers no longer whisper to the presence beside them in
   the dark, *O corpse-to-be* . . .

And yet perhaps this is the reason you cry,
this is the nightmare you wake screaming from:
being forever
in the pre-trembling of a house that falls.

3

In a restaurant once, everyone
quietly eating, you clambered up
on my lap: to all
the mouthfuls rising toward
all the mouths, at the top of your voice
you cried
your one word, *caca! caca! caca!*
and each spoonful
stopped, a moment, in midair, in its withering
steam.

Yes,
you cling because
I, like you, only sooner
than you, will go down
the path of vanished alphabets,
the roadlessness
to the other side of the darkness.

your arms
like the shoes left behind,
like the adjectives in the halting speech
of old men,
which once could call up the lost nouns.

4

And you yourself,
some impossible Tuesday
in the year Two Thousand and Nine, will walk out
among the black stones
of the field, in the rain,

and the stones saying
over their one word, *ci-gît, ci-gît, ci-gît,*

and the raindrops
hitting you on the fontanel
over and over, and you standing there
unable to let them in.

5

If one day it happens
you find yourself with someone you love
in a café at one end
of the Pont Mirabeau, at the zinc bar
where white wine stands in upward opening glasses,

and if you commit then, as we did, the error
of thinking,
one day all this will only be memory,

learn,
as you stand
at this end of the bridge which arcs,
from love, you think, into enduring love,
learn to reach deeper
into the sorrows
to come — to touch
the almost imaginary bones
under the face, to hear under the laughter
the wind crying across the black stones. Kiss
the mouth

which tells you, *here,*
here is the world. This mouth. This laughter. These temple
  bones.

The still undanced cadence of vanishing.

6

In the light the moon
sends back, I can see in your eyes

the hand that waved once
in my father's eyes, a tiny kite
wobbling far up in the twilight of his last look:

and the angel
of all mortal things lets go the string.

7

Back you go, into your crib.

The last blackbird lights up his gold wings: *farewell.*
Your eyes close inside your head,
in sleep. Already
in your dreams the hours begin to sing.

Little sleep's-head sprouting hair in the moonlight,
when I come back
we will go out together,
we will walk out together among
the ten thousand things,
each scratched too late with such knowledge, *the wages
of dying is love.*

T. S. Eliot

MARINA

Quis hic locus, quae regio, quae mundi plaga?

What seas what shores what grey rocks and what islands
What water lapping the bow
And scent of pine and the woodthrush singing through the fog
What images return
O my daughter.

Those who sharpen the tooth of the dog, meaning
Death
Those who glitter with the glory of the humming-bird,
  meaning
Death
Those who sit in the stye of contentment, meaning
Death
Those who suffer the ecstasy of the animals, meaning
Death

Are become unsubstantial, reduced by a wind,
A breath of pine, and the woodsong fog
By this grace dissolved in place

What is this face, less clear and clearer
The pulse in the arm, less strong and stronger—
Given or lent? more distant than stars and nearer than the eye

Whispers and small laughter between leaves and hurrying
  feet
Under sleep, where all the waters meet.

Bowsprit cracked with ice and paint cracked with heat.
I made this, I have forgotten
And remember
The rigging weak and the canvas rotten
Between one June and another September.
Made this unknowing, half conscious, unknown, my own.
The garboard strake leaks, the seams need caulking.

This form, this face, this life
Living to live in a world of time beyond me; let me
Resign my life for this life, my speech for that unspoken,
The awakened, lips parted, the hope, the new ships.

What seas what shores what granite islands towards my
    timbers
And woodthrush calling through the fog
My daughter.

The *Pearl* Poet

STANZAS FROM *PEARL*

1

Pearl all-pleasing, prince's treasure,
too chastely set in gold so pure!
From out the Orient, I aver,
ne'er proved I pearl its precious peer.
So round, so royal wherever ranged,
so sweetly small, so wondrous smooth;
where'er I judged of joyous gems,
I placed my Pearl apart, supreme.
I lost it—in a garden—alas!
Through glass to ground 'twas gone from me.
I pine, by Severing Love despoil'd
of Pearl mine own, without a spot.

Pearl, the fourteenth century alliterative middle English poem, is both an elegy and a vision occasioned by the death of the poet's infant daughter. The *Pearl* poet's use of the "dream" device that provides the poem's setting had been previously employed in the thirteenth century *Roman de la Rose*, as well as by Chaucer and Boccaccio—the latter of whose *Olympia* eclogue strikingly resembles *Pearl* (except for its more artificial tone, rhetorical emphasis, and Virgilian diction) in its elegiac depiction of Boccaccio's little daughter, Violante, now envisioned as a citizen of heaven. The use of the "pearl" to symbolize the state of purity and innocence derives from the Parable of the Pearl of Price (Matthew xiii). But it is also interesting to remember that the "pearl of the mind" was a phrase used by Chinese Buddhist priests to represent the "Buddah nature"; and to remember, too, that in the Syrian gnostic "Hymn of the Pearl" and in the *Zohar*, the "pearl" was an emblem of the soul itself. In *Pearl*, the Jungian idea of "the soul in search of its lost father" is reversed, so that it is now the father who is searching for his girl-child "pearl," as he attempts to accept and reconcile his loss according to the explanations of Christian doctrine. For this anthology I have included the first 32 of 101 stanzas in the translation by Sir Israel Gollancz.

2

There, in that spot, since hence it sped,
oft have I watch'd, wanting that gem
that once was wont to vanquish woe,
and raise my hap and all my weal.
It doth but pierce my heart with pangs,
my breast in bale but boil and burn;
yet ne'er me seem'd so sweet a song
as that still hour let steal to me.
    Yea, many a thought to me flow'd there,
    musing its charm so clad in clay.
    O earth! thou marrest a merry theme,
    Pearl mine own, without a spot.

3

From spot where such rich treasure wastes
fragrant spice must needs spring forth;
blossoms white and blue and red
shine there full sheer against the sun.
Flower and fruit shall know no flaw
where it down drave to earth's dark mould;
for from dead grain each blade must grow,
no wheat were else brought ever home.
    Each good from good is aye begun;
    so seemly a seed can never fail;
    ne'er fragrant spice shall cease to spring
    from that precious Pearl without a spot.

4

Unto the spot I picture forth
I enter'd into that garden green;
'twas August, at a festal tide,
when corn is cut with keen-edg'd hook.
The mound my Pearl had roll'd adown
with herbs was shadow'd, beauteous, bright,—
gilvers, ginger, and gromwell-seed,
and peonies powder'd all about.

But if the sight was sweet to see,
fair, too, the fragrance floating thence,
where dwelleth that glory, I wot full well,
my precious Pearl without a spot.

5

Before that spot my hands I clasp'd,
for care full cold that seized on me;
a senseless moan dinned in my heart,
though Reason bade me be at peace.
I plain'd my Pearl, imprison'd there,
with wayward words that fiercely fought;
though Christ Himself me comfort show'd,
my wretched will worked aye in woe.
  I fell upon that flowery plot;
    such fragrance flash'd into my brain,
    I slid into a slumber-swoon
    o'er that precious Pearl without a spot.

6

Thence, from that spot, my spirit sprang;
my body lay in trance on mound;
my soul, by grace of God, had fared
adventuring, where marvels be.
I knew not where that region was;
I was cast, I knew, where cliffs rose sheer.
Towards a forest I set my face,
where rocks so rich were to descry,
    that none can trow how rich the light,
    the gleaming glory glinting thence,
    for ne'er a web that mortals wove
    was half so wondrously bewrought.

7

Wondrously the hill-sides shone
with crystal cliffs that were so clear;
and all about were holt-woods bright,
with boles as blue as hue of Inde;
and close-set leaves on every branch
as burnish'd silver sway'd and swung;
when glided 'gainst them glinting gleams,
splendent they shone with shimmering sheen;
   and the gravel I ground upon that strand
   were precious pearls of Orient;
   the sunbeams were but dim and dark,
   if set beside that wondrous glow!

8

'Mid the magic of those wondrous hills
my spirit soon forgot all grief;
flavours of fruit so fresh were there,
as food full well they gave me strength;
birds in the wood together flew,
of flaming hues, both small and great;
nor citole-string nor citherner
could e'er re-tell their goodly glee;
   for when those birds did beat their wings,
   they sang with such a sweet accord,
   no rapture could so stir a man
   as to hear and see that wonderment.

9

All was so dight in wondrous wise,
no tongue of man hath power to tell
the beauty of that forest-land,
where fortune led me on and on.

Still forth I pressed in blissful mood;
no hill, though high, might hinder me.
Deeper in wood, more fair arose
plains and plants and spice and fruits,
   hedgerows and borders, and river-meads;
   as fine gold-thread were their steep banks.
   A water I reach'd that cleft the strand,—
   Lord, how wondrous was the sight!

10

The marvels of that wondrous flood!
Beauteous its banks with beryl bright;
with music sweet its waters swept;
with whispering voice it wander'd on.
And in the depths shone glittering stones;
as glint through glass they glimmer'd and glow'd;
as streaming stars in the welkin shine
on a winter night, when dalesmen sleep.
   Each pebble set there in that pool
   was an emerald, sapphire, or goodly gem,
   that all the water with light did gleam,—
   the glamour was so wondrous rare!

11

The wondrous glamour of down and dale,
of wood and water and noble plain,
stirr'd in me bliss, my bale allay'd,
scatter'd sorrow, pain destroy'd.
Along a stream I wended in joy,—
slowly it flow'd,—my mind was full;
the farther I follow'd those watery vales,
the mightier joy constrain'd my heart.
   Fortune fareth where she listeth,
   sends she solace, or sends she care;
   the wight on whom her will she worketh
   hath ever chance of more and more.

12

More was of wealth there, of this kind,
than I could tell, were leisure mine,
for earthly heart might not attain
unto the tenth of that glad Joy.
Certes, methought that Paradise
lay there beyond, o'er those broad banks.
The stream was some device, I trow'd,
Sir Mirth had made between great wells;
   beyond the brook, by hill or dale,
   the castle-bounds, I trow'd, were mark'd;
   but the water was deep, I durst not wade,
   and ever long'd I, more and more.

13

More and more, and yet still more,
I long'd to see beyond the brook;
for if 'twas fair where I then pass'd,
far fairer was the farther land.
About me stumbled I and stared;
to find a ford full hard I sought;
but perils more, iwis, there were,
the further I stalk'd along the bank;
   and ever methought I could not flinch,
   afeard, where wealth so winsome was;
   when new delights at hand were nigh,
   that moved my mind, e'en more and more.

14

More marvels then did daunt my soul;
I saw beyond that merry mere
a crystal cliff that shone full bright,
many a noble ray stood forth;
at the foot thereof there sat a child,—
so debonair, a maid of grace;

glistening white was her rich robe;
I knew her well, I had seen her ere.
  As gleaming gold, refin'd and pure,
  so shone that glory 'neath the cliff;
  long toward her there I look'd,—
  the longer, I knew her more and more.

15

The more I scann'd her face so fair,
her beauteous form when I had found,
such gladdening glory came to me
as seldom had been wont to come.
Longing me seized to call her name,
but wonder dealt my heart a blow;
I saw her in so strange a place,
well might the shock mine heart appal.
  Then lifted she her visage fair,
  as ivory pure her face was white;
  it thrill'd mine heart, struck all astray,
  and ever the longer, more and more.

16

More than me pleased was now my dread;
I stood full still, I dared not speak;
with open eyes and fast-closed mouth,
I stood as gentle as hawk in hall.
A ghostly vision I trow'd it was;
I dreaded what might there betide,
lest what I saw should me escape
ere I it held within my reach;
  when, lo! that spotless child of grace,
  so smooth, so small, so sweetly slight,
  arose in all her royal array,—
  a precious piece, bedight with pearls.

17

Choicest pearls, of sovereign price,
favour'd mortal there might see,
when all as fresh as a fleur-de-lys
adown that bank she came anon.
Gleaming white was her surcoat fine,
open at sides, and nobly edged
with pearls, the merriest, I trow,
than e'er I saw yet with mine eyes;
 ample the sleeves, I ween and wot,
 with double braid of pearl bedeck'd;
 her beauteous kirtle, matching well,
 with precious pearls was all bedight.

18

A crown that maiden wore, bedight
with margarites, and no stone else;
high pinnacled with clear white pearls,
with figured flowers wrought thereon.
No other tire was on her head;
her hair, too, hung about her neck;
her look was grave, as duke's or earl's;
whiter than whale-bone was her hue.
 Bright as clear gold her tresses shone,
 loose on her shoulders they softly lay;
 her glowing beauty had no lack
 of precious pearls on broid'ry dight.

19

The hems and wristbands were bedight,
at the hands, at sides, at openings,
with white pearl, and none other gem;
and burnish'd white her vesture was;

but a wondrous pearl, without a flaw,
amid her breast was firmly set;
soul of man would surely fail
ere mortal mind might mete its worth.
   No tongue might e'er avail, I trow,
   that sight to tell in fitting word,
     so fair was it, and clear, and pure,
     that precious pearl, where it was dight.

20

Bedight with pearls, that precious thing
came down the shore beyond the stream;
from here to Greece no gladder man
than I, when she was at the brink.
She was me nearer than aunt or niece,
wherefore my joy was much the more.
Proffer'd me speech that creature rare,
inclining low in womanly wise;
   her crown of richest worth she doff'd,
   and hail'd me with obeisance blithe.
     Well was me that e'er I was born,
     to answer that Sweet, in pearls bedight.

21

"O Pearl!" quoth I, "bedight in pearls,
art thou my Pearl, that I have plain'd,
bewept by me, so lone, a-night?
Much longing have I borne for thee,
since into grass thou hence didst glide;
pensive, broken, forpined am I;
but thou hast reach'd a life of joy,
in the strifeless home of Paradise.
   What fate hath hither brought my jewel,
   and me in dolorous plight hath cast?
     Since we were sunder'd and set apart,
     a joyless jeweller I have been."

22

That jewel there, so fair begemm'd,
up-rais'd her face, her eyes so grey,
put on her crown of Orient pearl,
and thus full gravely then she spake:
"Sir, thou hast misread thy tale,
to say thy Pearl is all perdu,
that is in chest so comely and strong
as in this garden of grace and glee;
    for ever to dwell and play herein,
      where miss and mourning come never nigh;
    this were thy treasure-hold, i' faith,
    wert thou a gentle jeweller.

23

"But, gentle sir, if thou must lose
thy joy for a gem that to thee was dear,
thou'rt set, methinks, on mad intent,
and carest for too brief a cause:
what thou didst lose was but a rose,
that flower'd and fail'd, as Nature bade;
through the casket's grace, enclosing it,
it now is proved a pearl of price.
    And thou hast call'd thy fate a thief,
      that ought from nought hath made for thee;
    thou blamest the balm of all thine ill,
    thou art a graceless jeweller."

24

A jewel to me was then this guest,
and jewels were her gentle words.
"Indeed," quoth I, "blest dearest mine,
my dire distress away thou draw'st.
I make request to be excused;
I trow'd my Pearl had pass'd from Day;

but now 'tis found, I shall make mirth,
and dwell with it in radiant groves,
   and praise my Lord and all His laws,
   who hath me brought this bliss anigh.
   Were I with thee beyond these waves,
   I were a joyful jeweller!''

25

"Jeweller!" said that purest gem,
"Why jest ye men? So mad ye are!
Three words thou spakest at one time;
thoughtless, forsooth, were all the three;
thou knowest not what one doth mean;
surely thy words outrun thy wit.
Thou sayest, thou deemest me in this dale,
because thou seest me with thine eyes;
   again, thou sayest, that in this land
   thyself wilt dwell with me e'en here;
   thirdly,—this stream would'st freely pass;
   this may no joyful jeweller.

26

"I hold that jeweller little to praise
that trusteth what with eye he seeth,
and much to blame and graceless he
that thinketh our Lord would speak a lie,
who leally promised to raise thy life,
though fortune gave thy flesh to death.
Full widdishins thou read'st His words,
thou trowest nought but what thou seest;
   and 'tis an overweening thing,
   that ill beseems each righteous man,
   to trow no tale be trustworthy,
   save his mere reason deem it so.

27

"Deem now thyself, if thou has dealt
such words as man to God should lift.
Thou sayest thou wilt dwell in this burgh;
'twere meet, methinks, first to ask leave;
and yet thou mightest miss the boon.
Thou wishest, too, to cross this stream;
first must thou reach another goal,—
colder thy corse must cling in clay;
   'twas forfeit in grove of Paradise;
   our forefather ill guarded it;
   through dreary death each man must pass,
   ere God deem right he cross this flood."

28

"Doomest thou me," quoth I, "my Sweet,
to dole again, I pine away.
Now have I found what I had lost,
must I forgo it, ere ever I end?
Why must I it both meet and miss?
My precious Pearl doth me great pain!
What serveth treasure but tears to make,
if one must lose it soon with woe?
   Now reck I ne'er how low I droop,
   how far men drive me from my land;
   when in my Pearl no part is mine,
   what is my doom but endless moan?"

29

"Thou deem'st of nought but doleful grief,"
said then that maid; "why dost thou so?
Through din of dole for losses small
many a man oft loseth more.

Rather shouldst thou cross thyself,
and praise aye God, in woe and weal;
anger avails thee not a cress;
who needs must bow, be not so bold;
   for though thou dance as any doe,
   chafe and cry in fiercest ire,
     since, to or fro, no way thou mak'st,
     thou must abide what He shall deem.

30

"Doom thou the Lord! Arraign Him still!
He will not swerve a foot from the way.
Thy mending 'mounteth not a mite,
though thou, for grief, be never blithe.
Stint from thy strife, and cease to chide,
and seek His grace full swift and sure;
thy prayer may His pity touch,
and Mercy may show forth her craft.
   His solace may assuage thy grief,
   that all thy losses glance lightly off;
     for, marr'd or made, mourning and mirth,
     all lieth in Him, as He deem fit."

31

Then deem'd I to that damosel:
"Let not my Lord be wroth with me,
if wildly I rave, rushing in speech,
my heart with mourning all was torn.
As welling water goeth from well,
I yield me to His mercy aye.
Rebuke me ne'er with cruel words,
my dear adored, e'en though I stray;
   but show me kindly comforting,
   piteously thinking upon this,—
     of care and me thou madest accord,
     that wast of all my bliss the ground.

32

"My bliss, my bale, hast thou been both;
but much the more my moan hath been;
since thou wast banish'd from ev'ry path,
I wist not where my Pearl was gone.
Now I it see, now less'neth my loss;
and when we parted, at one we were;
God forbid we be now wroth!
We meet so seldom by stock or stone.
  Though thou canst speak full courteously,
  I am but dust, and manners lack;
  the mercy of Christ, and Mary, and John,
  these are the ground of all my bliss."

Kenneth Rexroth

THE LIGHTS IN THE SKY ARE STARS
for Mary

Halley's Comet

When in your middle years
The great comet comes again
Remember me, a child,
Awake in the summer night,
Standing in my crib and
Watching that long-haired star
So many years ago.
Go out in the dark and see
Its plume over water
Dribbling on the liquid night,
And think that life and glory
Flickered on the rushing
Bloodstream for me once, and for
All who have gone before me,
Vessels of the billion-year-long
River that flows now in your veins.

The Great Nebula
of Andromeda

We get into camp after
Dark, high on an open ridge
Looking out over five thousand
Feet of mountains and mile
Beyond mile of valley and sea.
In the star-filled dark we cook
Our macaroni and eat
By lantern light. Stars cluster
Around our table like fireflies.
After supper we go straight
To bed. The night is windy
And clear. The moon is three days
Short of full. We lie in bed

And watch the stars and the turning
Moon through our little telescope.
Late at night the horses stumble
Around camp and I awake.
I lie on my elbow watching
Your beautiful sleeping face
Like a jewel in the moonlight.
If you are lucky and the
Nations let you, you will live
Far into the twenty-first
Century. I pick up the glass
And watch the Great Nebula
Of Andromeda swim like
A phosphorescent amoeba
Slowly around the Pole. Far
Away in distant cities
Fat-hearted men are planning
To murder you while you sleep.

The Heart of Herakles

Lying under the stars,
In the summer night,
Late, while the autumn
Constellations climb the sky,
As the Cluster of Hercules
Falls down the west
I put the telescope by
And watch Deneb
Move towards the zenith.
My body is asleep. Only
My eyes and brain are awake.
The stars stand around me
Like gold eyes. I can no longer
Tell where I begin and leave off.
The faint breeze in the dark pines,
And the invisible grass,
The tipping earth, the swarming stars
Have an eye that sees itself.

138

A Maze of Sparks of Gold

Spring — the rain goes by, the stars
Shine pale beside the Easter
Moon. Scudding clouds, tossing leaves,
Whirl overhead. Blossoms fall
In the dark from the fragrant
Madrone trees. You lie beside
Me, luminous and still in sleep.
Overhead bees sleep in their
Tree. Beyond them the bees in
The Beehive in the Crab drift
Slowly past, a maze of points
Of fire. I've had ten times your
Years. Time holds us both fixed fast
Under the bright wasting stars.

A Sword in a Cloud
of Light

Your hand in mine, we walk out
To watch the Christmas Eve crowds
On Fillmore Street, the Negro
District. The night is thick with
Frost. The people hurry, wreathed
In their smoky breaths. Before
The shop windows the children
Jump up and down with spangled
Eyes. Santa Clauses ring bells.
Cars stall and honk. Street cars clang.
Loud speakers on the lampposts
Sing carols, on juke boxes
In the bars Louis Armstrong
Plays *White Christmas*. In the joints
The girls strip and grind and bump
To *Jingle Bells*. Overhead
The neon signs scribble and
Erase and scribble again
Messages of avarice,
Joy, fear, hygiene, and the proud

Names of the middle classes.
The moon beams like a pudding.
We stop at the main corner
And look up, diagonally
Across, at the rising moon,
And the solemn, orderly
Vast winter constellations.
You say, "There's Orion!"
The most beautiful object
Either of us will ever
Know in the world or in life
Stands in the moonlit empty
Heavens, over the swarming
Men, women, and children, black
And white, joyous and greedy,
Evil and good, buyer and
Seller, master and victim,
Like some immense theorem,
Which, if once solved would forever
Solve the mystery and pain
Under the bells and spangles.
There he is, the man of the
Night before Christmas, spread out
On the sky like a true god
In whom it would only be
Necessary to believe
A little. I am fifty
And you are five. It would do
No good to say this and it
May do no good to write it.
Believe in Orion. Believe
In the night, the moon, the crowded
Earth. Believe in Christmas and
Birthdays and Easter rabbits.
Believe in all those fugitive
Compounds of nature, all doomed
To waste away and go out.
Always be true to these things.

They are all there is. Never
Give up this savage religion
For the blood-drenched civilized
Abstractions of the rascals
Who live by killing you and me.

Protoplasm of Light

How long ago
Frances and I took the subway
To Van Cortlandt Park. The people
All excited, small boys and
Cripples selling dark glasses.
We rushed to the open hills
North of the station as though
We'd be too late, and stood there
Hand in hand, waiting. Under
The trees the sun made little
Lunes of light through the bare branches
On the snow. The sky turned gray
And very empty. One by
One the stars came out. At last
The sun was only a thin
Crescent in our glasses with the
Bright planets nearby like watchers.
Then the great cold amoeba
Of crystal light sprang out
On the sky. The wind passed like
A silent crowd. The crowd sobbed
Like a passing wind. All the dogs
Howled. The silent protoplasm
Of light stood still in the black sky,
In its bowels, ringed with ruby
Fire, its stone-black nucleus.
Mercury, cold and dark like a
Fleck of iron, stood silent by it.
That was long ago.
Mary and I stand on the
Seashore and watch the sun sink

In the windy ocean. Layers
Of air break up the disc. It looks
Like a vast copper pagoda.
Spume blows past our faces, jellyfish
Pulse in the standing water,
Sprawl on the wet sand at our feet.
Twilight comes and all of the
Visible planets come out.
Venus first, and then Jupiter,
Mars and Saturn and finally
Mercury once more. Seals bark
On the rocks. I tell Mary
How Kepler never saw Mercury,
How, as he lay dying it shone
In his window, too late for him
To see. The mysterious
Cone of light leans up from the
Horizon into the pale sky.
I say, "Nobody knows what
It is or even where it is.
Maybe it is the great cloud
Of gas around the sun which
You will see some day if you
Are lucky. It stands out only
During an eclipse. I saw it
Long ago."

Blood on a Dead World

A blowing night in late fall,
The moon rises with a nick
In it. All day Mary has
Been talking about the eclipse.
Every once in a while I
Go out and report on the
Progress of the earth's shadow.
When it is passing the half,
Marthe and Mary come out
And we stand on the corner

In the first wisps of chilling
Fog and watch the light go out.
Streamers of fog reach the moon,
But never quite cover it.
We have explained with an orange,
A grapefruit, and a lamp, not
That we expect a four
Year old child to understand—
Just as a sort of ritual
Duty. But we are surprised.
"The earth's shadow is like blood,"
She says. I tell her the Indians
Called an eclipse blood on the moon.
"Is it all the blood on the earth
Makes the shadow that color?"
She asks. I do not answer.

William Blake

A LITTLE GIRL LOST

Children of the future Age
Reading this indignant page,
Know that in a former time
Love! sweet Love! was thought a crime.

In the Age of Gold,
Free from winter's cold,
Youth and maiden bright
To the holy light,
Naked in the sunny beams delight.

Once a youthful pair,
Fill'd with softest care,
Met in garden bright
Where the holy light
Had just remov'd the curtains of the night.

There, in rising day
On the grass they play;
Parents were afar,
Strangers came not near,
And the maiden soon forgot her fear.

Tired with kisses sweet,
They agreed to meet
When the silent sleep
Waves o'er heaven's deep,
And the weary tired wanderers weep.

To her father white
Came the maiden bright;
But his loving look,
Like the holy book,
All her tender limbs with terror shook.

"Ona! pale and weak!
"To thy father speak:
"O, the trembling fear!
"O, the dismal care!
"That shakes the blossoms of my hoary hair."

George Oppen

EXODUS

Miracle of the children   the brilliant
Children   the word
Liquid as woodlands   Children?

When she was a child I read Exodus
To my daughter   'The children of Israel . . .'

Pillar of fire
Pillar of cloud

We stared at the end
Into each other's eyes   Where
She said hushed

Were the adults   We dreamed to each other
Miracle of the children
The brilliant children   Miracle

Of their brilliance   Miracle
of